The Kiwi Beer Lover's Cookbook

Recipes by Sam Cook

P.O.Box 756, Orewa 0946, New Zealand
email: info@hurricane-press.co.nz

First published in 2009 by Hurricane Press Ltd,
PO Box 756, Orewa 0946, New Zealand

Copyright
Text © Sam Cook Enterprises Ltd
Design © 2009 Hurricane Press Ltd

Inspiration: Kelly, Goff and Tom (the adopted Kiwi)

National Library of New Zealand Cataloguing-in-Publication Data

Cook, Sam, 1980-
The Kiwi Beer Lover's Cookbook / recipes by Sam Cook.
Includes index.
ISBN 978-0-9864522-1-5
1. Cookery (Beer) 2. Cookery, New Zealand. I. Title.
641.6230993—dc 22

Printed by Bookbuilders, China

Distributed in New Zealand by
HarperCollins Publishers New Zealand
31 View Rd, Glenfield, Auckland 10

All rights reserved. No part of this publication may be reproduced, stored in a retrieval system, or transmitted in any form or by any means, electronic, mechanical, photocopying, recording or otherwise, without the prior permission of the publishers and copyright holders.

Photograph credits:
All photographs copyright © Hurricane Press Ltd with the exception of:
Cover (beer background): © Serban Anache | Dreamstime.com
Page 2: © Vincent Giordano | Dreamstime.com
Page 5: © Andrej Isakovic | Dreamstime.com
Page 21: © Anthony Boulton | Dreamstime.com
Page 77: © Gina Smith | Dreamstime.com

Foreword

While working on this book, I was often asked: why cook with beer? Some thought it was a gimmick. Others thought it would be fun. But few realised the role that beer plays in the cooking of good food.

Throughout my career as a chef, I've known many chefs who use beer as a 'special ingredient' to enhance dishes. Most people seem aware of wine's role in the kitchen but for some reason, beer's contribution remains almost a secret.

Beer has wonderful tenderizing properties and is a first-class marinade for many cuts of meat and fish. When roasting or grilling, beer can be used in basting sauces to add a richness to gravies. If used to simmer meats or vegetables, the beer helps bring out flavours.

While most of the alcohol evaporates during cooking, it leaves behind delicate flavours to enhance the meal.

In baking, beer creates a moist texture and can give food a longer shelf life.

The yeast in beer helps it act as a mild leavening agent, producing excellent breads and a fluffy batter perfect for frying. The flavours that make beer so enjoyable to drink transfer to food.

This collection of recipes uses beer to revamp some of New Zealand's classic dishes and some that are influenced by our multicultural cuisine. It is not a gourmet cookbook. All meals have been tested in a household kitchen.

Finally, I urge you to take a relaxed attitude towards your cooking. Experiment with different styles and brands of beer. Find what works best for you – that's the fun of cooking.

Keep it real!

Sam

'He was a wise man who invented beer.'
- *Plato*

Cooking with beer

The recipes in this book have been designed to help you have fun in the kitchen, as well as cook some great food. These guidelines will help you do both.

Types of Beer

Each recipe recommends a style of beer to be used – lager, draught or dark. They should be used at room temperature unless the recipe states otherwise. These terms have been used to reflect the most common styles of beer consumed in New Zealand.

Lager: in New Zealand, lagers are medium in body and light in colour. For this book, the term includes premium lagers.

Draught: this term describes what is classed in New Zealand as 'brown beer' but is not a lager. Draught beers are amber, reddish-brown or copper-coloured and medium-bodied. They contain a noticeable degree of caramel-type malt character in flavour and often in aroma.

Dark: this describes types of beer, including stouts, porters and those closely related to these, in which the beer is full-bodied, distinctly darker in colour and slightly more roasty or caramel flavoured than draughts.

Choosing Beers

You are urged to experiment and use your favourite beers. While this will be fun, and you'll get different flavours and outcomes with each beer, you should be aware it's well-established that some types of beer work best in different situations.

For instance, light breads work best with sweet lagers. On the other hand, some dark beers can become quite bitter in taste when used as a reduction in some dishes. As a general rule, go with the beers that would drink well with the type of food.

Skill Levels

The recipes in this book have been created for novices but also those with more experience. Preparation times have been estimated within a range because people work at different speeds. Work at the speed you feel comfortable – cooking is not a race.

Cooking Times

Cooking times are also estimated within a range because cooking is not an exact science – sometimes it simply takes longer than planned!

The oven times have been stated for standard ovens but if you have a fan-forced oven, please adjust temperatures in line with manufacturer's instructions.

Alcohol Content

Though alcohol is heat-sensitive and can be cooked out of the food, you should still be considerate when cooking for guests and advise them their meal contains beer.

Safety

Above all, it's important to cook safely.

Never leave cooking unattended. Always watch the pan or pot when cooking with oil or fat. If oil or fat is smoking, turn off the heat. Snuff out a fat fire with a pot lid or oven tray.

Don't cook while under the influence of alcohol.

Contents

Starters	7
Breads & muffins	21
Soups	39
Vegetables & salads	51
Sauces & marinades	63
Something fishy	77
Stews & casseroles	93
Meats & mains	107
Sweet as	127
Index	142

The meaning of life

A New Zealand professor of philosophy was explaining to students the meaning of life. Raising a large glass jar to the lectern, the professor filled it with rocks until no more could fit.

'Is the glass full?' the professor asked. The students agreed it was.

The professor produced a bag of small pebbles and tipped them into the jar. They tumbled between the rocks and settled, filling the few gaps that remained.

'Now is the glass full?' the professor asked.

Less certain this time, the students said they thought it was. The professor then produced a bag of sand, emptying it into the mouth of the jar. The sand found its way into every crack left between the rocks and the pebbles.

The professor asked once more: 'Is the glass full?' The class emphatically agreed it was.

The professor smiled and said it was time the students understood the meaning of life.

'Imagine this jar is your life. The rocks are the big things in your life – your loved ones, your relationships, your health. The pebbles are the things that are important – like your job or your car – but they're not as important as the rocks. And the sand is just everything else that gets into your life – it's not important but it's always there.

'To lead a full life, you need to make sure you put the rocks in first. If you fill your life with sand, there'll be no room for the really important things. And that is the meaning of life.'

As he finished, a young student stepped forward and pulled a bottle of beer from his bag. He removed the cap and poured the beer into the jar. The beer soaked into the sand, and around the rocks and pebbles, until it was all in the jar. The student turned to the amazed class.

'The moral of this story,' the student explained, 'is that no matter how full your life is, you can always find room for a beer.'

Starters

Blue Cheese Dip

Serves:	4-6
Preparation:	15-20 mins
Cooking:	3-4 mins
Refrigeration:	1 hour minimum

200ml beer (lager) – chef's tip: Mac's Gold
200gm mild Cheddar cheese grated
100gm blue cheese – chef's tip: Kapiti Kikorangi
2 tablespoons butter
2 cloves garlic crushed
1 small onion finely diced
1 teaspoon Worcestershire sauce

Bowl: grate the Cheddar cheese and crumble the blue cheese into the bowl. Stand until the cheeses have reached room temperature.

Saucepan: heat the beer over medium-high heat until it just starts to bubble. Remove from heat.

Bowl: using an electric mixer, combine the cheeses with all the ingredients except the beer. With the mixer running, gradually pour in the beer until a smooth dip is achieved.

Container: store in a sealed container and refrigerate for at least 1 hour before serving.

Serving up

Bread or sticks of celery and raw carrot are a good match.

Crab Dip

Serves:	6
Preparation:	10-15 mins
Refrigeration:	1 hour minimum

30ml beer (lager) – chef's tip: Export Gold
1 cup mayonnaise
½ teaspoon mild English mustard
¼ teaspoon hot pepper sauce – chef's tip: Kaitaia Fire
½ teaspoon lemon juice or to taste
170gm crab meat, fresh or tinned
1 teaspoon fresh parsley chopped
Salt and cracked black pepper to season

Bowl: mix the beer, mayonnaise, mustard, pepper sauce and lemon juice in a bowl. When smooth, stir in the crab meat followed by the parsley. Season with salt and black pepper. Refrigerate for at least 1 hour.

Serving up

Crackers or toasted bread go well with this dip.

Cheese & Spinach Dip

Serves:	4
Preparation:	10-15 mins
Cooking:	5-10 mins

160ml beer (lager) – chef's tip: Speight's Summit
3 cups mild Cheddar cheese grated
2 tablespoons all-purpose flour
½ cup spinach chopped
1 tablespoon fresh coriander chopped
Hot pepper sauce (optional) to taste – chef's tip: Kaitaia Fire
Salt and cracked black pepper to season

Saucepan (medium): bring the beer to the boil over a medium heat. Reduce heat and slowly stir in the cheese and flour. Stir until the cheese is fully melted but do not allow the mixture to bubble.

Mix in the spinach, coriander, salt and pepper. If you like your dips spicy, add hot pepper sauce to taste.

Serving up

Best served slightly warm with lightly toasted bread or your favourite corn chips.

Kumara & Coriander Dip

Serves:	6
Preparation:	10-15 mins
Cooking:	20-25 mins

60ml beer (draught) – chef's tip: Speight's Gold Medal Ale
3 cloves garlic
2 golden kumara peeled and cut into 2cm cubes
2 medium carrots peeled and cut into 2cm cubes
½ cup vegetable stock
1 tablespoon olive oil
Salt and cracked black pepper to season
2 tablespoons fresh parsley chopped
2 tablespoons fresh coriander chopped

Oven: preheat your oven to 180°C. Place the unpeeled garlic cloves on a non-stick oven tray and bake for 10 minutes or until soft. Remove and stand to cool.

Pots (2): boil the kumara and carrots in separate pots until soft. Drain. Allow to cool.

Blender: squeeze in the baked garlic, discarding its peel, and add the kumara and carrots. Add the beer and half of the stock and process. With the motor running, add the olive oil. Process until the puree is smooth, adding enough of the remaining stock to achieve the desired texture. Season with salt and pepper.

Serving up

Serve the dip at room temperature. Stir in the parsley and coriander just before serving. Goes well with raw vegetables or bread sticks.

Bean Dip

Serves:	6-8
Preparation:	5-10 mins
Cooking:	20-25 mins

120ml beer (lager) – chef's tip: Monteith's Golden
1 tablespoon oil
½ cup onion roughly diced
½ cup red capsicum roughly diced
2 cloves garlic crushed
1 420gm tin tomatoes chopped
1 420gm tin red kidney beans drained and rinsed
4 slices jalapeno pepper
½ cup fresh coriander chopped
1 cup mild Cheddar cheese grated
Salt and cracked black pepper to season

Garnish (optional)

Sour cream
Red capsicum slices
Coriander leaf

This is a yummy party dip or appetiser before dinner.

Saucepan: over a low-medium heat, sweat the onions in the oil for about 2 minutes. Add the capsicum and cook for 2 minutes. Add the garlic and cook for a further 2 minutes, stirring well.

Add the beer and increase the temperature to high. Once the mixture reaches boiling, allow it to boil for 1 minute. Add the tomatoes and bring back to the boil. Immediately reduce the heat and leave to simmer for 5 minutes.

Add the kidney beans, stirring well, and bring the mixture back to boiling. Reduce heat to simmer for 5 minutes or until the mixture has thickened but not dried out.

Add the slices of jalapeno pepper and coriander. Mix through.

Blender or food processor: transfer and blend until the dip has almost reached a smooth consistency. Season with salt and pepper. Add the grated cheese, working it into the mix until it has fully melted.

Serving up

Serve warm. Garnish with a small spoon of sour cream and a couple of slices of red capsicum and leaf of coriander saved from the ingredients.

Serve with corn chips or baked flour tortillas.

Cheese & Onion Dip

Serves:	12
Preparation:	5-10 minutes
Refrigeration:	1½ hours minimum

80ml beer (lager) – chef's tip: Export Gold
225gm cream cheese
225gm sour cream
32gm packet onion soup mix – chef's tip: Maggi

Bowl: stand the cream cheese until it reaches room temperature and then beat until it becomes fluffy. Add the beer and beat until smooth. Stir in the sour cream and onion soup mix.

Refrigerate for at least 1½ hours. Stir before serving.

Serving up

Dish up this party dip with plenty of potato or corn chips, or raw vegetables.

Cheese Fondue

Serves:	4
Preparation:	10-15 mins
Cooking:	8-10 mins

180ml beer (lager) – chef's tip: Steinlager Pure
1 clove garlic halved
2 cups Gruyere (or similar) cheese grated
1 cup tasty Cheddar cheese grated
1 tablespoon all-purpose flour

Dipping food

Cubes of white bread, chicken, meat and raw vegetables all go well when speared and dipped.

Saucepan (medium): chop the clove of garlic in half and smear the inside of the pan. When it is coated, add the beer and what's left of the garlic. Over a low-medium heat, gently warm the beer. Discard the garlic when the beer is warm but not boiling.

Bench: gently mix the grated cheeses together and coat with the flour. Gradually add the cheese to the beer, stirring continuously. Let the mixture thicken but do not overheat. Reduce the heat whenever the mixture starts to bubble.

Fondue pot: transfer the mixture to a fondue pot and keep warm over a burner. Use forks or spears to coat your dipping foods with the cheese mix. If the texture gets too thick, add small amounts of warmed beer.

If you don't have a fondue pot, you can improvise by serving in small warmed bowls, regularly transferring mixture from your pan.

Classic Cheese on Toast

Serves:	4
Preparation:	10-15 mins
Cooking:	15-18 mins

250ml beer (lager) warm – chef's tip: Mac's Gold
50gm butter
4 tablespoons all-purpose flour
250gm tasty Cheddar cheese grated
2 teaspoons mild English mustard
2 tablespoons Worcestershire sauce
½ teaspoon cracked black pepper
4 large slices of bread
Butter for toast

Saucepan: melt the butter and add the flour, stirring continuously for 2 minutes. Gradually add the warm beer and continue to stir until a smooth, sticky sauce is formed.

Add the grated cheese and stir until it is melted. Mix in the mustard, Worcestershire sauce and black pepper. Stir well.

Toaster: lightly toast the slices of bread and butter.

Grill: generously smother each slice of toast with the cheese mix and place under the grill for as long as it takes for the cheese to bubble and for the surface to turn a golden brown.

Stuffed Tomatoes

Makes:	10
Preparation:	30-40 mins
Cooking:	20 mins

100ml beer (lager) – chef's tip: Export Gold
10 large tomatoes
Salt and cracked black pepper to season
1 420gm tin whole corn kernels drained
1 small onion finely diced
1 green capsicum finely diced
200gm Cheddar cheese grated
3 cups fresh bread crumbs
1 tablespoon olive oil

Oven: preheat to 180°C.

Bowl: cut the tops off the tomatoes and transfer the pulp with a teaspoon to the mixing bowl. Season the inside of the hollowed tomatoes. Add all the other ingredients to the bowl, except the beer, and start to stir. Gradually introduce the beer, stirring well, until you achieve a firm texture.

Fill the hollowed tomatoes with the mixture. Lightly brush the tomato skins with olive oil.

Oven: place the tomatoes on a baking tray and bake for about 20 minutes.

Serving up

Allow the tomatoes to cool for a few minutes as they retain heat and can burn if served straight from the oven.

Salsa

Makes:	2½ cups
Preparation:	30-40 mins
Refrigeration:	20 mins minimum

100ml beer (lager) – chef's tip: Steinlager Pure
400gm fresh tomatoes finely chopped
¾ cup red onions finely diced
1 large clove garlic crushed
½ teaspoon table salt
¼ teaspoon ground black pepper
Juice of 1 fresh lime (while lime is recommended, lemon can be substituted)
¼ cup fresh coriander chopped

Bowl (large): combine finely chopped tomatoes, diced red onions, crushed garlic, salt, pepper, lime juice and beer. Add the chopped coriander and mix through. Marinate in the refrigerator for at least 20 minutes. Drain most of the liquid just before serving.

Serving up

Salsa is the perfect accompaniment to many dishes or terrific just with corn chips.

Mushroom Platter

Makes:	10
Preparation:	20-25 mins
Cooking:	45-55 mins

70ml beer (draught) – chef's tip: Lion Red
2½ tablespoons olive oil
1 clove garlic crushed
45gm butter
1 tablespoon oil
5 cups of onions thinly sliced
¼ teaspoon salt
1½ teaspoons fresh thyme chopped
1 teaspoon brown sugar
¼ cup toasted pine nuts
10 large flat mushroom caps
3 rashers bacon cooked and diced
125gm Brie or Camembert cheese cut into 10 slices

Bowl (small): mix the 2½ tablespoons of olive oil and the crushed garlic to infuse. Set aside.

Saucepan (large, non-stick): over low-medium heat, melt the butter with the 1 tablespoon of oil. Add the onions and saute over medium heat for 5 minutes until they are soft. Reduce to low heat and add the salt, thyme and sugar. Stir regularly and cook for 25-30 minutes until the onions are caramelised. Add the beer, stirring it into the onions and allowing it to be absorbed. When the beer is completely absorbed, stir in the pine nuts. Set aside.

Oven: preheat to 200°C.

Baking tray (non-stick or greased): lightly brush both sides of the mushrooms with the mix of oil and garlic. Place the mushroom caps top-up in a single layer.

Oven: bake for 8-10 minutes until the caps begin to shrink. Remove from the oven and turn the caps over. Fill them with the onion mixture and bacon pieces. Top with a slice of cheese. Return to the oven for 5-7 minutes. Remove and serve while hot.

Chicken Wings with Salsa

Serves:	4-6
Preparation:	40-60 mins
Refrigeration:	overnight
Cooking:	40-45 mins

Marinade

660ml beer (lager) – chef's tip: Mac's Gold
2 teaspoons dried thyme
4 tablespoons fresh coriander roughly chopped
4-6 cloves garlic sliced
Peel from 2 lemons with each peel split in half
Salt and cracked black pepper

Wings

24 chicken wings

Salsa – see recipe on page 14

Garnish

1 spring onion finely sliced

It's happened to most of us – the mates are coming over to watch the game and your dilemma is what to serve up. The beers are easy. The food less so. You want good-tasting finger food but don't want to spend the whole game in the kitchen.

These chicken wings are ideal as most of the preparation can be done the night before the match.

Marinade

Bowl (large): place the wings in the bowl and sprinkle with thyme, coriander, garlic, lemon peel, salt and pepper. Pour the beer over the chicken wings and toss them to coat them in the marinade.

Cover with plastic wrap and refrigerate overnight. If you get the chance, turn the wings in the marinade an hour or two before you plan to cook them.

Remove the wings from the marinade, taking care to make sure none of the garlic, coriander or lemon peel has stuck to them.

Wings

Oven: preheat to 190°C.

Baking dish: place the wings in a single layer in the dish and bake for 40-45 minutes, turning them occasionally.

Salsa (see recipe on page 14)

Serving up

Serve with a bowl of salsa and garnish with sliced spring onion.

Grilled Chicken Satay

Serves:	6
Preparation:	10-15
Refrigeration:	overnight
Cooking:	7-10 mins

Marinade

120ml beer (lager) – chef's tip: Mac's Gold
¼ cup smooth peanut butter
½ cup light coconut milk
1 tablespoon fresh coriander chopped
1 tablespoon crystalised ginger
2 cloves garlic crushed
½ teaspoon red chilli finely chopped and deseeded

Chicken

900gm chicken breasts

Sauce

125ml beer (lager) – chef's tip: Mac's Gold
½ cup smooth peanut butter
½ cup sugar
3 tablespoons light soy sauce
1 clove garlic crushed
½ teaspoon red pepper flakes
¼ teaspoon sesame oil

Bowl: cut the chicken into bite-sized chunks.

Blender: for the marinade, combine the beer, peanut butter, coconut milk, coriander, ginger, garlic and chilli. Process.

Container: pour the marinade over the chicken. Turn the chicken cubes until the meat is well coated. Cover and refrigerate overnight to marinate.

BBQ or grill: thread the chicken cubes on skewers (if wooden, make sure they are soaked in water for 30 minutes before use to stop them catching alight) and grill over medium heat, turning often until the chicken is cooked.

Saucepan: for the sauce, combine the ingredients in the saucepan, stirring with a wooden spoon. Heat over a low-medium heat, stirring regularly to ensure the sauce is smooth and warmed through. The sauce will continue to thicken when removed from the heat. This recipe makes about 1 cup of sauce.

Serving up

Serve the peanut sauce over the skewers.

Avocado Wedges

Serves:	4
Preparation:	2-2¼ hours
Cooking:	5-10 mins

250ml beer (lager) – chef's tip: Export Gold
1 cup all-purpose flour
2 cloves garlic crushed or finely chopped
1½ teaspoons paprika
2 avocadoes peeled and cut into wedges
Salt and cracked black pepper to season
Vegetable oil for deep frying
8 small cherry tomatoes halved (optional)
2 tablespoons chives chopped (optional)

Salsa – see recipe on page 14

Bowl: combine the beer, flour, garlic and paprika in a bowl. Leave to stand for 2 hours.

Bench: cut the avocadoes into wedges – but not too thin. Lightly season with salt and pepper and coat them with the batter.

Deep fryer: preheat oil to 180°C in your deep fryer, or if using stove top fryer, heat the oil until a cube of bread crisps easily and quickly. Fry the wedges in hot oil for about 3 minutes or until they are golden brown. Remove and drain on paper towels. Season again with salt and pepper.

Serving up

Avocadoes always go well with tomato so try serving them with salsa or small cherry tomatoes, with chopped chives.

Deviled Eggs

Serves:	6
Preparation:	15-20 mins
Cooking:	5-10 mins

1 tablespoon beer (lager) – chef's tip: Monteith's Golden
6 eggs
1 teaspoon white vinegar
1 tablespoon mayonnaise
½ teaspoon Worcestershire sauce
¼ teaspoon salt
¾ teaspoon mild mustard
Cracked black pepper to season
6 olives pitted (optional)
Fresh parsley (optional garnish)

Saucepan: hard-boil the eggs for no longer than 10 minutes and cool. Peel and halve, using a wet knife to avoid sticking. Scoop out the yolks and place in a mixing bowl. Set aside the whites.

Bowl: add the beer and remaining ingredients, except the olives, to the yolks and mix well.

Carefully scoop the mix into the egg whites to create 12 deviled eggs.

Serving up

Add half an olive to the top of each egg or garnish with a sprinkling of chopped parsley (optional) and cracked pepper.

Prawn Fritters

Makes:	about 14
Preparation:	10-15 mins
Cooking:	5-6 mins each batch

125ml beer (lager) – chef's tip: Steinlager Pure
¾ cup self-raising flour
Salt and cracked black pepper to season
1 egg lightly beaten
300gm cooked prawns peeled and deveined
2 spring onions finely sliced
Oil to shallow fry

Bowl: sift the flour with salt and pepper into a bowl. Form a well and pour in the beer and lightly beaten egg. Stir until the batter is smooth. Chop the prawns and add to the batter. Stir in the sliced spring onions.

Fry pan (large): heat enough oil to cover the bottom of your pan over medium heat. Create fritters by spooning 1 tablespoon of the batter mix into the pan, spreading it evenly.

Cook each fritter for about 3 minutes on each side or until golden brown.

Corn Fritters

Makes:	about 18
Preparation:	10-15 mins
Cooking:	5-6 mins each batch

125ml beer (lager) – chef's tip: Steinlager Pure
2 cups self-raising flour
1 teaspoon baking powder
1 teaspoon ground cumin
Salt and pepper to season
2 eggs
½ cup sweet chilli sauce
2 cups frozen sweetcorn (thawed)
2 tablespoons chives chopped
Oil to shallow fry

Bowl 1: sift in the flour, baking powder, cumin, salt and pepper. Mix well.

Bowl 2: combine the eggs, beer, sweet chilli sauce, corn and chives. Mix well. Transfer the contents to Bowl 1 and mix thoroughly.

Fry pan (large): heat enough oil to cover the bottom of your pan over medium heat. Spoon 1 tablespoon of the fritter mixture into the pan, spreading it evenly. Cook for about 3 minutes each side until golden brown.

Breads and muffins

The World's Easiest Bread

Makes:	1 loaf
Preparation:	5-10 mins
Cooking:	45-50 mins

330ml beer (any)
3 cups self-raising flour
1 teaspoon salt

The yeast in beer works wonders with bread – and you'll struggle to find a simpler way to make bread than this.

Oven: preheat to 180°C.

Bowl (large): sift the flour into the bowl (it's essential to sift the flour – don't skip this step). Add the salt. Form a well in the top of the flour and pour in the beer. The beer and flour will start to froth. Mix well with a wooden spoon.

Loaf tin: transfer the dough to a greased loaf tin.

Oven: bake for 45 minutes or until the crust sounds hollow when lightly tapped. Remove and stand to cool on a rack.

Whole Wheat Bread

Makes:	1 loaf
Preparation:	10-15 mins
Cooking:	50-55 mins

330ml beer (lager or draught) – chef's tip: Monteith's Golden
1½ cups all-purpose flour
1½ cups whole wheat flour
4½ teaspoons baking powder
1½ teaspoons salt
5 tablespoons brown sugar

Oven: preheat to 180°C.

Bowl (large): combine all the dry ingredients and mix well. Add the beer and stir until your dough is ready.

Loaf tin: transfer the dough to a greased loaf tin.

Oven: bake for 50-55 minutes or until the crust sounds hollow when lightly tapped. Remove and stand to cool on a rack.

Cheese & Onion Bread

Makes:	1 loaf
Preparation:	10-15 mins
Cooking:	1½-1¾ hours

330ml beer (any) – chef's tip: Waikato Draught
3 cups self-raising flour
1½ teaspoons salt
3 tablespoons sugar
1 cup tasty Cheddar cheese grated
4 spring onions finely chopped

Oven: preheat to 180°C.

Bowl (large): sift the flour into the bowl and combine with all the ingredients except the beer. Form a well and add the beer. Mix well.

Loaf tin: transfer the dough to a greased loaf tin.

Oven: bake for 1½ hours or until the crust sounds hollow when lightly tapped. Remove and stand to cool on a rack.

Basil Bread

Makes:	1 loaf
Preparation:	5-10 mins
Cooking:	45-50 mins

330ml beer (lager) – chef's tip: Speight's Summit
3 cups self-raising flour
½ cup fresh basil chopped
1 teaspoon salt
1 tablespoon olive oil

Oven: preheat to 180°C.

Bowl (large): sift the flour into the bowl. Add the chopped basil and salt. Mix the dry ingredients. Form a well in the top of the flour and pour in the beer. The beer and flour will start to froth. Mix well with a wooden spoon.

Loaf tin: transfer the dough to a greased loaf tin.

Oven: bake for 45 minutes or until the crust sounds hollow when lightly tapped. To brown the top, brush olive oil on the crust 10 minutes before it's ready. Remove and stand to cool on a rack.

Rye bread

Makes:	2 loaves
Preparation:	20-25 mins
Stand time 1:	overnight
Stand time 2:	1½ hours
Cooking:	25-35 mins

330ml beer (dark) – chef's tip: Speight's Distinction Ale
2 cups rye flour
16gm dry yeast
2 tablespoons white sugar
1 tablespoon salt
2 tablespoons shortening
1 egg
1 tablespoon pumpkin seeds (optional)
3 cups all-purpose flour
3 teaspoons baking powder
1 tablespoon olive oil

Bowl 1 (large): combine the rye flour, yeast and beer in the bowl. Cover with plastic wrap and leave out overnight – not in the refrigerator. Next day, add the sugar, salt, shortening and egg. Using your hands and a wooden spoon, blend the mix until smooth. It will take some effort but it's worth it. Add pumpkin seeds, if you like them. Add the all-purpose flour and baking powder, cup by cup, until you have soft dough that is not sticky.

Board: knead on a floured board for about 7-10 minutes.

Bowl 2: pour the dough into an oiled bowl and brush the surface with oil. Leave in a warm place to let the dough rise. It should increase in size in about 1 hour. Break into loaves and place on a baking tray covered with baking paper. Let the dough rise for 30 minutes.

Oven: preheat to 200°C. Bake for 30 minutes. Remove to cool.

Sun-dried Tomato Bread

Makes:	1 loaf
Preparation:	10-15 mins
Cooking:	1-1¼ hours

330ml beer (draught) – chef's tip: Lion Red
3½ cups self-raising flour
¼ cup sugar
1 egg
¼ cup tomato sauce
60gm sun-dried tomatoes cut into 1cm pieces

Oven: preheat to 180°C.

Bowl (large): sift the flour and sugar into a bowl and mix well. Form a well and pour in the beer, egg and tomato sauce. Mix well.

When satisfied with the dough, fold in the sun-dried tomatoes.

Loaf tin: transfer the dough to a greased loaf tin.

Oven: bake for about 1 hour or until the crust sounds hollow when lightly tapped. Remove and stand to cool on a rack.

Savoury Swirl Bread

Makes:	1 loaf
Preparation:	5-10 mins
Cooking:	45-50 mins

330ml beer (dark) – chef's tip: Black Mac
3 cups self-raising flour sieved
1 teaspoon salt
1½ teaspoons yeast extract – chef's tip: Marmite
Pumpkin seeds
1 tablespoon olive oil

Oven: preheat to 180°C.

Bowl (large): sift the flour into the bowl (it's essential to sift the flour – don't skip this step). Add the salt. Form a well in the top of the flour and pour the beer into it.

The beer and flour will start to froth. Mix well with a wooden spoon. Add the yeast extract and work it through the dough so it forms the appearance of a swirl. When happy with your dough, roll it in pumpkin seeds..

Loaf tin: transfer the dough to a greased loaf tin and sprinkle a few more pumpkin seeds on top.

Oven: bake for 45 minutes or until the crust sounds hollow when lightly tapped. To brown the top, brush olive oil on the crust 10 minutes before it's ready. Remove and stand to cool on a rack.

Herb Bread

Makes:	1 loaf
Preparation:	12-15 mins
Cooking:	45-50 mins

330ml beer (lager) – chef's tip: Export Gold
3 cups all-purpose flour
2 tablespoons baking powder
2 tablespoons sugar
¼ cup ground flaxseed
1 teaspoon salt
1 teaspoon dried basil
1 teaspoon dried rosemary
1 teaspoon dried thyme
1 tablespoon olive oil

Oven: preheat to 180°C.

Bowl (large): mix all the dry ingredients, making sure to sift the flour into the bowl. Form a well and pour in the beer and oil. Mix well with a wooden spoon.

Loaf tin: transfer the dough to a greased loaf tin.

Oven: bake for about 45 minutes or until the crust sounds hollow when lightly tapped. Remove and stand to cool on a rack.

Sourdough Starter

1 cup all-purpose flour
1 cup warm water

Sourdough starter is easy to make but it takes a week before it becomes an active ingredient in bread. It can be kept in the refrigerator and topped up weekly to help make plenty of bread.

Bowl (large, non-metal): to start, mix the flour and warm water with a wooden spoon. At no stage, allow the starter to come into contact with metal.

Container (sealed, plastic): store in a warm place (ideal temperature is 20-23°C). Every 24 hours, remove half the mixture and replace with half a cup of flour and half a cup of warm water.

The mixture should start to bubble and give off a beery smell between 3 and 7 days of starting.

When it has developed a bubbly froth, it's ready to store in the refrigerator. It needs to breathe so either use a lid with a hole or do not tightly fit the lid.

To keep the starter alive, you need to reduce it by half and top it up once a week with half a cup of flour and half a cup of warm water. You will often find a beery fluid forming around the starter. Either drain it or mix it in if the starter is a bit dry. Look after it and your starter will last indefinitely.

Whenever you want to make sourdough bread, add a cup of flour and a cup of warm water to the starter. Mix, leave out of the refrigerator, covered with plastic wrap, and wait for fermentation to take place. It could take 2-8 hours to ferment but it's ready when it has become spongy in appearance and coated with froth.

The longer you leave the starter to ferment, the more sour your bread will taste.

Take the amount of starter you need for your bread recipe and return the rest to the refrigerator for future use.

Sourdough Bread

Makes:	2 loaves
Preparation:	10-15 mins
Stand time:	2¼ hours
Cooking:	45-50 mins

250ml beer (lager) room temperature – chef's tip: Steinlager Pure
1 cup sourdough starter (see opposite page)
½ cup sugar
5 cups all-purpose flour

The hoppy taste of beer helps make terrific sourdough bread but it's best with lager as dark ales tend to produce bread that's too sweet or malty.

First, you need to make what's called 'sourdough starter' – a concoction that actually lives in your fridge and makes your bread rise. To make your starter, see the opposite page. Once you have your batch of starter, here's how to make great sourdough bread.

Bowl (large): combine the beer and the sourdough starter in the bowl. Stir in the sugar until it has dissolved. Mix in enough flour to make a dough you can knead with your hands.

Board: turn the dough onto a floured board and knead for about 10 minutes. Whenever the dough becomes sticky, sift a bit more flour onto the board.

Bowl: place the dough in an oiled bowl and flip so the top is also oiled. Cover with a slightly damp clean tea towel. Leave to sit in a warm place for 1½ hours.

Board: turn the dough onto the floured board and knead for 5 minutes.

Loaf tins: divide the dough into two loaf tins and shape into loaves. Cover again with the tea towel and allow the dough to rise for about 45 minutes. Each loaf should significantly increase in size.

Oven: preheat to 180°C. Bake bread for about 45 minutes or until the crust sounds hollow when tapped. Remove and allow to cool on a rack.

Sourdough bread can be frozen and reheated later.

Serving up

Tear it into chunks and serve with soup or gravy-laden stews.

Pizza Crust

Makes:	2 x 40cm pizzas
Preparation:	30-40 mins
Stand time:	2 hours
Cooking:	15-20 mins (pizza)

150ml beer (draught) – chef's tip: Lion Red
2 teaspoons sugar
1½ teaspoons active dry yeast
2 tablespoons olive oil
1 medium egg at room temperature, lightly beaten
2½ cups all-purpose flour
¼ teaspoon salt

A wonderful thing about beer as a cooking ingredient is its yeast content. As well as helping to make tasty breads, beer gives pizza dough an extra twist.

This recipe provides enough dough to make two thin crust bases (40cm each).

Saucepan: heat the beer and sugar over low heat for a few minutes, until the sugar melts but before the beer starts to boil. Remove from the heat and sprinkle the active dry yeast over the surface of the beer. Wait about 10 minutes while the yeast dissolves and the liquid turns foamy. When cooled, mix in the olive oil and egg.

Bowl 1: sift the flour and salt into a bowl and mix well. Form a well. Pour in the contents of the saucepan and mix with a wooden spoon. As soon as the ingredients are combined, start working the mixture with your hands. Turn out onto a board dusted with flour and knead for 7-10 minutes or until the dough becomes smooth and pliable.

Bowl 2: lightly oil this bowl. Place the dough in the bowl, turning it to ensure it becomes oiled on all sides. Cover the bowl with plastic wrap and leave in a warm place for 2 hours allowing the dough to increase in size.

Oven: preheat to 200°C.

Board: lightly dust the surface of the board. Punch down the dough, divide it into two pieces and roll them into pizza bases, adding more dusting flour as required.

Oven: after adding your favourite toppings, and pizza sauce (see recipe on page 76), bake your pizza for about 20-25 minutes or until the crust is crisp.

Pizza Crust with Pizza Sauce (see page 76) ▶

Pepperoni Bread

Makes:	1 loaf
Preparation:	20-25 mins
Stand time:	1¾ hours
Cooking:	20-25 mins

120ml beer (lager) – chef's tip: Export Gold
3-3¼ cups self-raising flour
1 teaspoon active dry yeast
½ cup warm water
½ tablespoon sugar
½ tablespoon salt
⅛ cup hard cheese grated (such as Parmesan or Romano)
½ tablespoon garlic powder
1 teaspoon dried oregano
1 teaspoon dried rosemary
¾ teaspoon ground black pepper
75gm pepperoni finely chopped
½ tablespoon oil
½ egg white

Bowl 1 (large): sift ½ cup of flour and the yeast into the bowl and mix. Add warm water and the beer. Stir well. Cover with plastic wrap and stand in a warm place for 15-20 minutes.

Add the sugar, salt, cheese, garlic powder, dried oregano, dried rosemary and black pepper.

Mix well and start adding the flour a cup at a time. Stir well and when the dough becomes too heavy to stir, start kneading the mixture with your hands. Continue adding flour until the dough pulls away from the side of the bowl.

Knead for about 15 minutes, pulling the dough into pieces, folding them and using flour to prevent sticking. When the dough is smooth and pliable, fold in the pepperoni, trying to evenly distribute the pieces of meat.

Bowl 2: place the dough in an oiled bowl and turn to coat the rest of the surface with oil. Cover with plastic wrap and stand in a warm place for up to 1 hour, while it increases in size.

Oven: preheat to 180°C.

Shape the dough into a loaf shape on a baking tray covered with baking paper. Allow the dough to rise again for about 30 minutes. Brush the top of the dough with egg white to get a glazed finish to the crust.

Oven: bake for 20-25 minutes or until the crust sounds hollow when lightly tapped. Remove and stand to cool on a rack.

Serving up

This is the ideal bread to serve with cheese and pickles.

Cheese Muffins

Makes:	4 jumbo muffins
Preparation:	10-15 mins
Cooking:	15-20 mins

330ml beer (lager) – chef's tip: Monteith's Golden
3 cups all-purpose flour
5 teaspoons baking powder
½ teaspoon salt
1 tablespoon sugar
1 cup Cheddar cheese grated
3 tablespoons butter melted

Oven: preheat to 180°C.

Bowl (large): combine the flour, baking powder, salt and sugar in a bowl and mix. Form a well and pour in the beer. Stir well.

Muffin tray: pour mixture into greased hollows, filling each to ¾ full to allow the muffins to rise when baking.

Brush the tops of the muffin mixture with butter and sprinkle cheese on the top.

Oven: bake for 15-20 minutes or until browned. Remove and stand to cool on a rack.

Oatmeal Muffins

Makes:	6 jumbo muffins
Preparation:	12-18 mins
Cooking:	20-25 mins

330ml beer (lager or draught) – chef's tip: Tui
1½ cups all-purpose flour
4 teaspoons baking powder
1½ teaspoons salt
½ cup sugar
2 cups rolled oats
50gm butter softened
2 eggs

Oven: preheat to 180°C.

Bowl 1 (large): sift the flour, baking power, salt and sugar into a bowl. Mix in the rolled oats. Cut in the softened butter and mix again.

Bowl 2: in a separate bowl, beat the eggs with the beer. Stir this mixture into Bowl 1. Work the mixture until all ingredients are fully blended.

Muffin tray: spoon the mixture into greased hollows, filling each to ¾ full to allow the muffins to rise when baking.

Oven: bake for 20-25 minutes or until browned. Remove and stand to cool on a rack.

Bran Muffins

Makes:	5-6 jumbo muffins
Preparation:	10-15 mins
Cooking:	30-35 mins

100ml beer (any) – chef's tip: DB Draught
2 cups All-Bran cereal
200ml milk
1¼ cups all-purpose flour
½ cup sugar
1 tablespoon baking powder
¼ teaspoon salt
1 egg
¼ cup vegetable oil

Oven: preheat to 200°C.

Bowl 1 (large): combine the All-Bran cereal with the beer and milk and leave to stand for 5 minutes.

Bowl 2 (medium): sift in the flour, sugar, baking powder and salt.

Bowl 3 (small): beat the egg with the oil.

Pour the contents of bowls 2 and 3 into the large bowl containing the All-Bran mixture. Stir only until all the contents are combined.

Muffin tray: pour mixture into greased hollows, filling each to ¾ full to allow the muffins to rise when baking.

Oven: bake for 30-35 minutes or until golden brown. Remove and stand to cool on a rack.

Savoury Muffins

Makes:	6 jumbo muffins
Preparation:	30-35 mins
Cooking:	25-30 mins

330ml beer (lager) – chef's tip: Export Gold
3 cups all-purpose flour
2 tablespoons sugar
1 tablespoon baking powder
1 teaspoon salt
1 teaspoon dried basil
½ teaspoon pepper
½ teaspoon garlic powder
½ cup vegetable oil
1 egg
1 small onion finely chopped
½ cup ham or cooked bacon pieces
½ cup tasty Cheddar cheese grated
1 egg white mixed with 1 tablespoon water

Oven: preheat to 175°C.

Bowl 1 (large): sift in the flour, sugar, baking powder, salt, basil, pepper, and garlic powder. Make a well.

Bowl 2 (medium): whisk together the beer, oil, egg and onion. Pour this mixture into the well in Bowl 1. Stir only until all the contents are combined. Fold in the pieces of ham or bacon, and the cheese, trying to evenly distribute these.

Muffin tray: pour mixture into greased hollows, filling each to ¾ full to allow the muffins to rise when baking.

Bowl 3 (small): beat the egg white with water. Brush over the top of the muffins and allow to stand for 10 minutes before baking.

Oven: bake for 25-30 minutes or until golden brown. Remove and stand to cool on a rack.

Fruit & Raisin Bread

Makes:	1 loaf
Preparation:	20-30 mins
Cooking:	1½-1¾ hours

330ml beer (lager or draught) – chef's tip: Tui
2 cups brown sugar
60gm butter
3 eggs
½ teaspoon vanilla extract
4½ cups all-purpose flour
2 tablespoons baking powder
1½ cups raisins
1½ cups dried mixed fruit

Oven: preheat to 180°C.

Saucepan (large): combine the beer, sugar and butter in the saucepan over a low-medium heat. When the ingredients melt and blend, remove from the heat and allow to cool.

Bowl (small): beat the eggs and add the vanilla extract. Pour into the saucepan when the beer mixture has cooled.

Bowl (large): sift in the flour and baking powder and add the raisins and mixed fruits. Mix and form a well. Slowly pour in the beer mixture. Stir well to evenly distribute the raisins and fruit.

Loaf tin: transfer the dough to a greased loaf tin.

Oven: bake for 1½ hours or until a skewer pushed into the centre of the loaf emerges dry and clean. Remove and stand to cool on a rack.

'Beer is proof that God loves us and wants us to be happy.'

- Benjamin Franklin

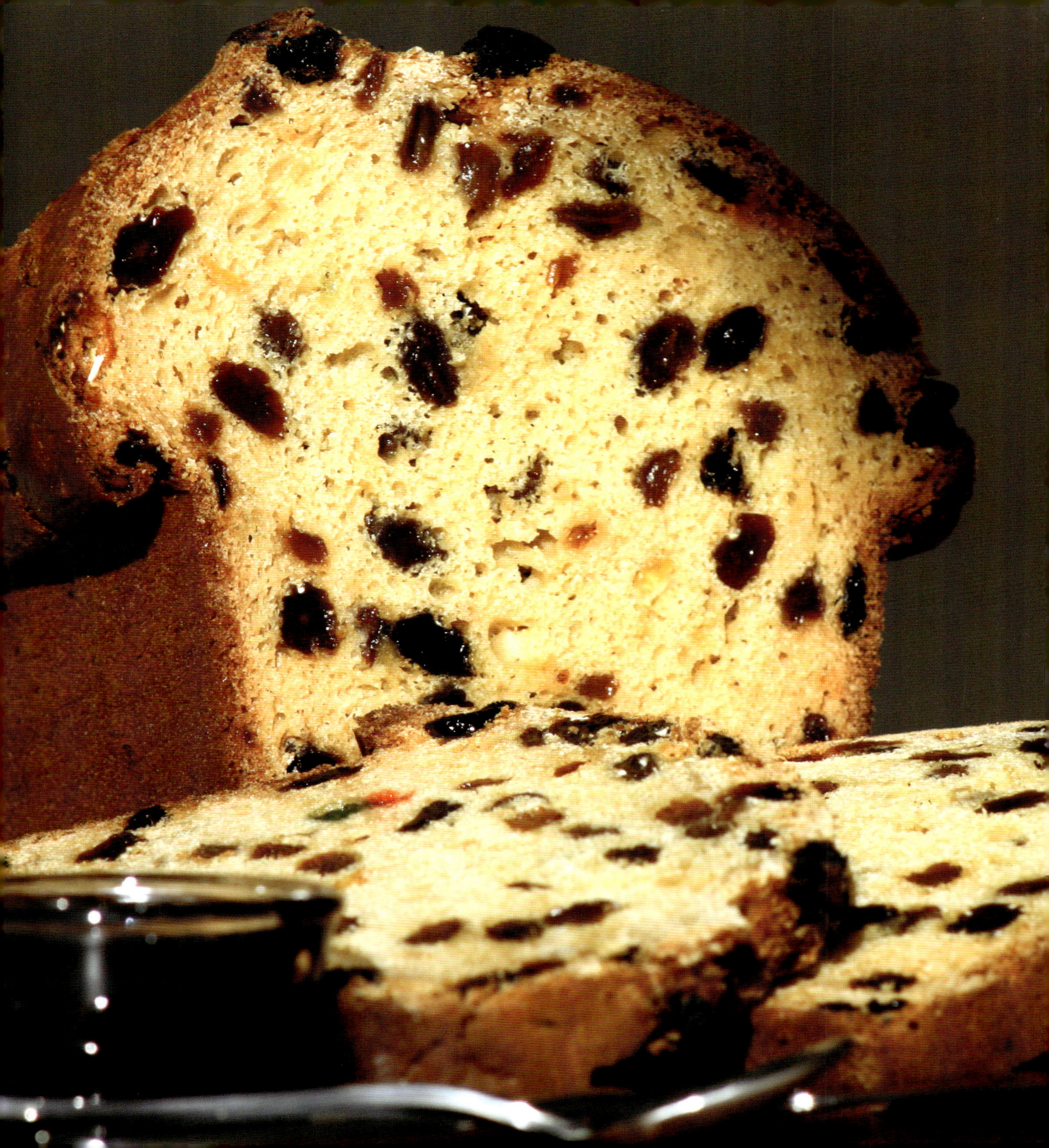

Banana, Date & Walnut Bread

Makes:	1 loaf
Preparation:	25-30 mins
Cooking:	1-1¼ hours

240ml beer (dark) – chef's tip: Black Mac
1 cup brown sugar
½ cup bananas mashed
1 egg
½ teaspoon vanilla extract
1 tablespoon vegetable oil (optional)
1½ cups all-purpose flour
1 teaspoon baking powder
½ teaspoon salt
¾ teaspoon ground cinnamon
Pinch ground allspice
½ teaspoon ground cardamom (optional)
½ teaspoon ground cloves
¾ cup walnuts chopped
1 tablespoon all-purpose flour
1 cup dates pitted and chopped
1 tablespoon fresh ginger crushed

Oven: preheat to 180°C.

Bowl 1 (large): combine the brown sugar, bananas, egg and vanilla extract in the bowl. If you want more moist bread, add the oil.

Bowl 2: sift in the flour, baking powder, salt, cinnamon, allspice and cloves. If you want a more gingery taste, add in the cardamom. Mix.

Transfer the flour mix from Bowl 2 to Bowl 1 a spoonful at a time, adding beer as you do, and stir until fully blended.

Toss the walnuts in the remaining tablespoon of flour. Add these and the dates and ginger to the bread mix and blend.

Loaf tin: transfer the dough to a greased loaf tin.

Oven: bake for 1 hour or until a skewer pushed into the centre of the loaf emerges dry and clean. Remove and stand to cool on a rack.

Soups

Pumpkin, Pear & Chilli Soup

Serves:	4 as a starter
Preparation:	10-15 mins
Cooking:	35-45 mins

125ml beer (lager) – chef's tip: Export Gold
½ fresh red chilli thinly sliced and deseeded
1 420gm tin pears in juice (not syrup) drained
1 tablespoon oil
½ medium onion roughly chopped
2 cloves garlic sliced
4 cups pumpkin skinned and cubed
4 cups vegetable stock
Salt and cracked black pepper to season

Oven: preheat to 180°C.

Baking dish (non-stick): sprinkle the sliced chilli over the drained pears.

Oven: bake the pears for 5 minutes. Remove from oven and stand to cool.

Soup pot (large): over low-medium heat, heat the oil and sweat the onion and garlic until soft and translucent. Add the pumpkin and cook for 2 minutes. Add the pears and chilli and cook for 2 more minutes, mixing well. Add the beer and stock. Bring to the boil. Reduce the heat to low and simmer for 25-30 minutes or until the pumpkin is tender.

Blender or food processor: process until the soup is smooth. Season with salt and pepper.

Cream of Mushroom Soup

Serves:	6 as a starter
Preparation:	10-15 mins
Cooking:	40-45 mins

125ml beer (lager) – chef's tip: Export Gold
1 tablespoon oil
1 medium onion roughly sliced
2 cloves garlic crushed
1kg button mushrooms sliced
2 tablespoons fresh thyme
2 tablespoons lemon juice
2¾ cups chicken stock
¾ cup cream
Salt and cracked black pepper to season
½ tablespoon fresh parsley chopped
Cracked black pepper

Soup pot (large): heat the oil over low-medium heat and sweat the onion and garlic until soft and translucent. Add the mushrooms, thyme and lemon juice and heat over medium heat for 10-15 minutes or until the liquid released by the mushrooms disappears.

Add the beer and stock to just cover the mushrooms and bring to the boil. Immediately reduce the heat to low and simmer for 20 minutes. Transfer to a blender or processor.

Blender or food processor: process to a coarse puree. Return to the pot and add the cream. Bring back to the boil. Remove from the heat and return to the blender. Process to a smooth consistency. Season with salt and pepper and serve.

Serving up

Garnish with chopped parsley and cracked black pepper.

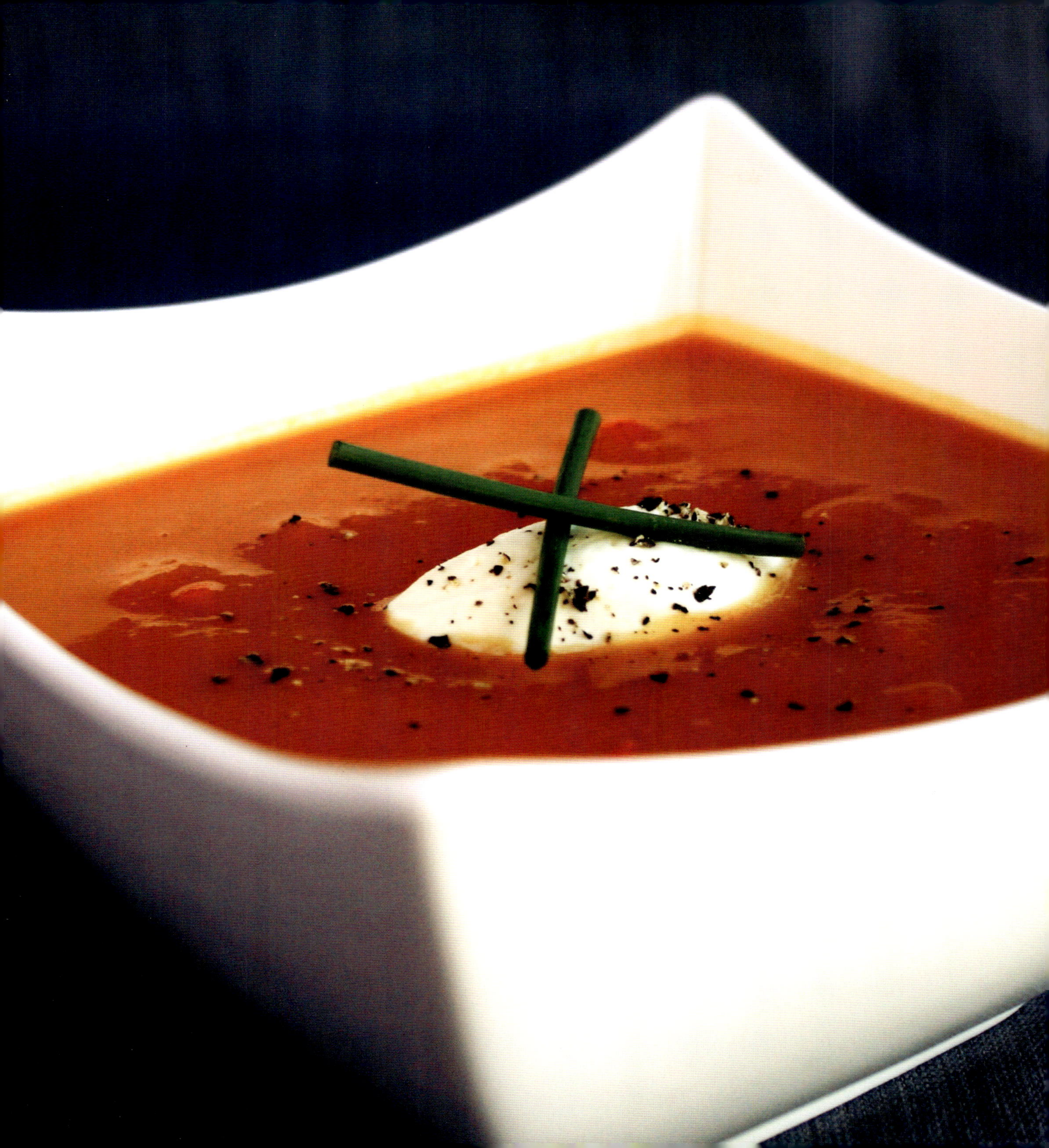

Kumara & Curried Apple Soup

Serves:	4-6
Preparation:	30-40 mins
Cooking:	40-50 mins

330ml beer (lager) – chef's tip: Mac's Gold
¼ cup dark raisins
60gm butter
1 teaspoon oil
1 medium onion diced
2 apples cored and diced but not peeled
1 tablespoon curry powder
2 teaspoons fresh ginger crushed
2 tablespoons all-purpose flour
3-4 cups chicken or vegetable stock
½ cup apple juice concentrate – chef's tip: Fresh Up Crisp Apple
1 stick cinnamon
1 teaspoon tamari soy sauce
2 medium kumara peeled and diced
Salt and cracked black pepper to season
1 lemon cut into wedges (optional)

Bowl 1 (covered): soak the raisins in the beer in a covered bowl for at least 30 minutes or overnight if you have the opportunity.

Saucepan (medium): over medium heat, melt the butter with the oil and saute the onion until it has sweated and is translucent. Add the apples and saute for 3-4 minutes until they are softened.

Sprinkle the curry powder over the mix and reduce the heat to low-medium. Cook for about 8 minutes, stirring often. Stir in the ginger and cook for 2 more minutes.

Bowls 1 and 2: while the onion and apples are cooking, drain the raisins, reserving the beer in Bowl 2 and raisins in Bowl 1.

Saucepan: sift the flour into the pan over the onion and apple mixture and stir over low heat for 1 minute. Gradually add the beer, stirring to avoid lumps, and cook for 5-7 minutes until the mixture is smooth and free of the taste of flour.

Blender or food processor: blend the contents of the saucepan and add the raisins. Process until smooth.

Soup pot (large): combine the stock, apple juice concentrate, cinnamon stick and soy sauce. Bring to the boil and add the kumara. Reduce the heat, cover and simmer for about 30 minutes or until the kumara is tender. Remove the cinnamon stick from the pot and pour in the contents of the apple, raisin and beer puree.

Check for taste – you may want to add more apple juice concentrate if you prefer it sweeter. Season with salt and cracked black pepper.

Serving up

You may wish to add a teaspoon of sour cream or creme fraiche to each bowl. A wedge of lemon on the side also helps with this dish.

Bacon Hock & Vegetable Soup

Serves:	4
Preparation:	20-30 mins
Stand time:	overnight + 1 hour
Cooking:	3½-4½ hours

180ml beer (lager or draught) – chef's tip: Tui
220gm green split peas rinsed and drained
2 tablespoons oil
1 onion diced
1 medium carrot peeled and diced
1 stick celery diced
600ml cold water
1 small potato peeled and diced (120gm)
2 tablespoons fresh parsley chopped
1 teaspoon fresh thyme chopped
¼ teaspoon mustard powder
½ tablespoon cider vinegar
1 bacon hock (800gm-1kg)
Salt and black pepper to season

Pot (medium): soak the split peas in a pot of cold water overnight.

Heat the peas in the same water over a medium-high heat until boiling. Allow to boil for 2 minutes and remove from the heat. Cover and leave to stand for 1 hour.

Soup pot (large): heat the oil over low-medium heat and add the onion, carrot and celery. Cook for 5-7 minutes, stirring often, until the onion is soft. Add the 600ml of cold water, beer, potato, parsley, thyme, mustard powder, cider vinegar and the bacon hock (whole).

Drain the split peas and add them to the soup pot. Bring the soup to the boil and immediately reduce the heat to low. Simmer, covered, for 3-4 hours, stirring occasionally.

When the peas are tender, remove the bacon hock. Cut away the skin and fat. Cut the pieces of bacon from the bone and return them to the pot. Discard the bone. It has added flavour to the soup and has served its purpose. Warm through and simmer for 10 minutes before serving.

Season with salt and pepper.

Serving up

Serve with your favourite bread.

Onion Soup

Serves:	4-6
Preparation:	30-35 mins
Cooking:	50-60 mins

250ml beer (dark) – chef's tip: Monteith's Black
2 tablespoons butter unsalted
3 large onions sliced
2 large red onions sliced
4 shallots finely chopped
2 cloves garlic crushed
1-2 tablespoons brown sugar
2 bay leaves
1 teaspoon dried basil
1 teaspoon dried thyme
3 cups beef stock
Salt and cracked black pepper to season
1 cup cheese grated

Soup pot (large): melt the butter over a low-medium heat and add the onions, shallots and garlic. Cook for 10-15 minutes until they are soft but have not turned brown. Add the sugar and stir for 2 minutes.

Add the bay leaves, basil, thyme, stock and beer.

Bring to the boil. Immediately reduce heat to low and simmer, covered, for 25-30 minutes or until the onions are tender. Season with salt and pepper and if you prefer this soup sweeter, add a bit more sugar. Remove and discard the bay leaves.

Oven grill: preheat.

Soup bowls (ovenproof): ladle the soup into bowls and sprinkle with grated cheese. Place under the hot grill for 2-3 minutes or until the cheese has melted and turned golden brown.

Serving up

Be careful – the soup bowls will be very hot when they come out from under the grill.

ONION SOUP

Seafood Gumbo

Serves:	4
Preparation:	15-20 mins
Cooking:	1-1¼ hours

90ml beer (lager) – chef's tip: Mac's Gold
6 tablespoons all-purpose flour
6 tablespoons oil
2 cloves garlic crushed
1 medium onion diced
½ cup green capsicum roughly diced
½ cup red capsicum roughly diced
2 bay leaves
¼ teaspoon cayenne pepper
¼ teaspoon salt
1 dozen oysters and their juice
3 cups fish stock
½ 420gm tin tomatoes chopped half-drained
350gm white fish fillets – chef's tip: snapper or another firm white fish
225gm raw prawns peeled and deveined
¼ cup fresh parsley chopped
Salt and cracked black pepper to season

Gumbo is a thick soup that's a meal in itself. Do not underestimate how filling it can be.

Soup pot (large): combine the oil and flour, whisking well. When blended, cook over a medium heat, stirring constantly, until the mixture starts to brown. Add the garlic, onion, capsicums, bay leaves, cayenne pepper and salt. Mix well.

Simmer, uncovered, for 10-15 minutes.

Add the juice from the oysters, the stock, tomatoes and beer. Mix well. Simmer, uncovered, for 30 minutes.

Cut the fish fillets into strips of about 7-8cm. Add them and cook for 3 minutes.

Add the prawns and cook for 3 minutes. Add the oysters and cook for 4-5 minutes.

Mix in the parsley, stir the gumbo and cover the pot. Remove it from the heat and allow to stand for 5 minutes.

Remove the bay leaves and season with salt and black pepper.

Serving up

Offer a slice of thick crunchy bread on the side with a dab of butter. A good choice of bread is sourdough (see recipe on page 29).

Broccoli & Blue Cheese Soup

Serves:	4 as a starter
Preparation:	10-15 mins
Cooking:	20-25 mins

200ml beer (lager) – chef's tip: Export Gold
1 tablespoon oil
1 medium onion chopped
1 clove garlic crushed
1 large potato peeled and cubed
3¼ cups vegetable stock
1 head of broccoli (300gm-400gm) chopped into small pieces
50gm creamy blue cheese crumbled
50gm creamy blue cheese crumbled (optional garnish)

Soup pot (large): heat the oil over low-medium heat and sweat the onion until soft and translucent. Add the garlic and stir for 1-2 minutes. Add the potato, beer and vegetable stock. Stir and bring to the boil. Immediately reduce heat and simmer, covered, for about 10-15 minutes or until the potato is tender.

Add the broccoli. Bring to the boil. Reduce heat and simmer, uncovered, for about 5 minutes until the broccoli is tender but remains bright green.

Blender or food processor: transfer the soup to a blender and crumble in half the cheese (50gm). Blend to a smooth texture.

Serving up

Pour into soup dishes and if you want more bite as well as a burst of colour, crumble in the extra 50gm of blue cheese, swirling it on the surface of the soup.

Leek & Potato Soup

Serves:	4 as a starter
Preparation:	10-15 mins
Cooking:	35-40 mins

250ml beer (lager) – chef's tip: Mac's Gold
2 leeks finely chopped
50gm butter
2 cloves garlic crushed
3 cups vegetable stock
2 tablespoons celery diced
1 teaspoon mustard seed
4 large potatoes peeled and cut into 2cm cubes
½ cup cream
Salt and pepper to season
½ teaspoon fresh chervil chopped

Prepare the leeks by cutting off their tops and cutting them down their centre lengthways and wash thoroughly. Chop the leeks finely.

Soup pot (large): heat the butter over a low-medium heat and lightly saute the leeks with the garlic for 5-7 minutes. Add the beer, stock, celery, mustard seeds and potatoes. Bring to the boil. Reduce heat and simmer for 30-35 minutes until the potatoes are tender.

Blender or food processor: blend to a coarse puree. Return to the pot and stir in the cream. Reheat for 1-2 minutes. Season with salt and pepper. Serve.

Serving up

Garnish with chopped chervil.

Roast Tomato & Garlic Soup

Serves:	4
Preparation:	15-20 mins
Cooking:	45-55 mins

125ml beer (lager) – chef's tip: Steinlager Pure
Oil for brushing
1 garlic bulb
2kg ripe tomatoes halved with cores removed
Salt and cracked black pepper to season
2 teaspoons caster sugar
2 tablespoons oil
1 medium onion finely chopped
2½ cups vegetable stock

Garnish

Enough whole small tomatoes on the vine to sit in the serving bowl (see photograph), optional

This soup can be visually spectacular as well as tasty.

Oven: preheat to 180°C.

Baking tray: lightly brush the garlic bulb with oil and place the whole bulb and tomatoes, cut side up, on a tray lined with baking paper. Season with salt and pepper and sprinkle with sugar.

Oven: roast for 30-40 minutes or until the tomatoes and garlic are tender. Remove from oven for 10 minutes.

When cool enough, peel the tomatoes over a bowl, discarding the skin but keeping their juice. Squeeze the garlic from its bulb. Set aside.

Soup pot (large): heat the oil over a low-medium heat and sweat the onions until soft. Add the garlic and cook for 2 minutes. Add the tomatoes and their juice. Bring to the boil.

Add the beer and vegetable stock and bring back to the boil. Reduce heat and simmer, uncovered, for 20 minutes stirring occasionally. Season with salt and pepper.

Blender or food processor: process until smooth. Pass the soup through a sieve into a bowl, extracting the tomato seeds and discarding them. Return the soup to the pot and bring back to the boil. Simmer for 10 minutes or until the soup reaches your desired level of thickness.

Serving up

If you want to present this soup with flair, roast whole small tomatoes on the vine, lightly brushed with oil, for 5 minutes before sitting them in the serving bowls.

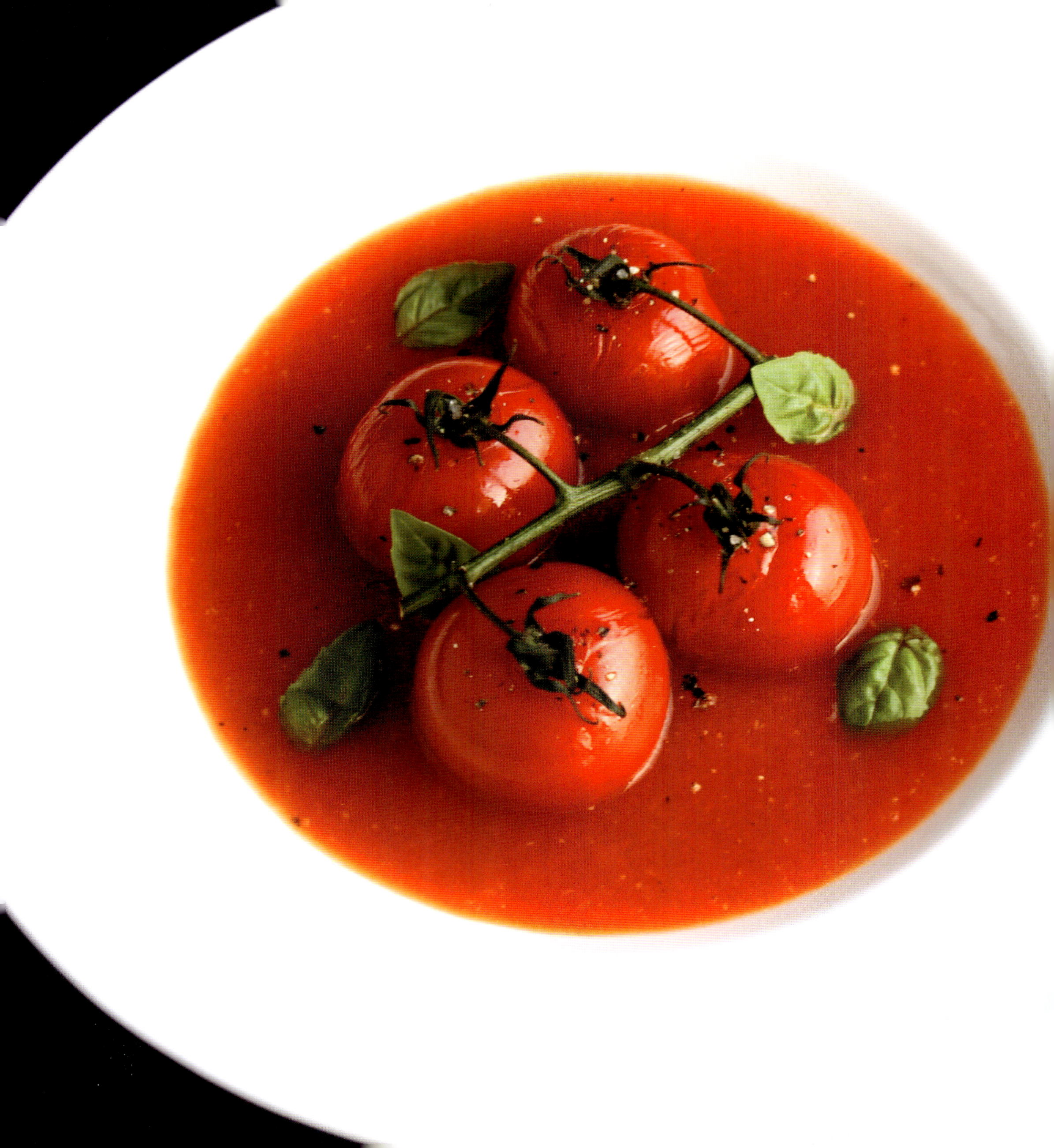

Black Bean & Chorizo Soup

Serves:	6
Preparation:	15-20 mins
Stand time:	6 hours minimum
Cooking:	2-2½ hours

330ml beer (dark) – chef's tip: Monteith's Black
450gm dried black beans rinsed
2 tablespoons oil
1 large onion diced
200gm chorizo sausage diced
4 cloves garlic crushed
1 red capsicum diced
1 stick celery diced
2 teaspoons ground cumin
½ teaspoon ground chilli powder
1 420gm tin tomatoes diced (drained)
2 teaspoons brown sugar
5 cups chicken stock
1 bouquet garni
Salt and cracked black pepper to season

Garnish

6 teaspoons sour cream (optional)
2 fresh limes cut into wedges
1 cup fresh coriander chopped (optional)

To prepare the beans, they should be soaked in 3-4 litres of cold water for at least 6 hours or preferably overnight. Drain and rinse them.

Pot (large): cover the beans with water and bring to the boil. Maintain the heat to keep them on the boil for 10 minutes. Remove from heat. Drain and rinse and set aside for 5 minutes.

Soup pot (large): heat the oil over medium heat and add the onion. Saute it for 2-3 minutes. Add the chorizo sausage, stirring for 3 minutes. Add the garlic and stir for 2 minutes.

Add the red capsicum, the celery, ground cumin, chilli powder, tomatoes and sugar. Add the beans, beer, chicken stock and the bouquet garni.

Bring to the boil. Reduce heat and simmer, stirring occasionally, partially covered, for 1½-2 hours or until the beans are tender.

Season with salt and pepper.

Serving up

Ladle into bowls and garnish with a dollop of sour cream. Provide fresh lime juice to be added to the soup to taste. Chopped coriander can also be sprinkled on the top.

Vegetables and salads

Sesame Green Beans

Serves:	4
Preparation:	10-15 mins
Cooking:	10-15 mins

330ml beer (lager) – chef's tip: Monteith's Golden
3 tablespoons soy sauce
3 teaspoons lime juice
1 teaspoon white sugar
1 cup all-purpose flour
¼ cup sesame seeds
Vegetable oil for deep frying
350gm fresh green beans
Salt to season

Deep fryer: heat the oil to 190°C.

Bowl (small): combine the soy sauce, lime juice and sugar. Whisk to form a dipping sauce for the beans.

Bowl (medium): sift the flour into the bowl and mix in the sesame seeds. Form a well and add the beer. Mix until smooth.

Rinse and trim the beans. Roll them in the batter until evenly coated. Shake off any excess.

Deep fryer: fry the beans in batches for 1-2 minutes or until golden brown. Drain them on paper towels and add salt to taste.

Vegetable Stir-Fry

Serves:	4
Preparation:	10-15 mins
Cooking:	10-15 mins

60ml beer (lager) – chef's tip: Export Gold
2 tablespoons oil
2 cloves garlic crushed
2 small onions, quartered
1 tablespoon fresh ginger finely chopped
230gm tin water chestnuts drained
250gm broccoli cut into florets
250gm cauliflower cut into florets
1 small bunch spinach
½ cup baby corn
¼ cup hot chicken stock
100gm bean sprouts
3 spring onions sliced

Fry pan (large) or wok: heat the oil over low-medium heat. Add the garlic, onions and ginger, stirring them into the oil for 1 minute. Add the rest of the vegetables, except for the bean sprouts, combining them well.

Add the beer and the stock, stirring all the time. Bring to the boil and cover. Cook for 3-4 minutes or until the vegetables are tender. Check every minute or so that the vegetables are not sticking to the pan. Toss in the bean sprouts just before serving.

Serving up

Serve with rice or egg noodles. Garnish with sliced spring onions.

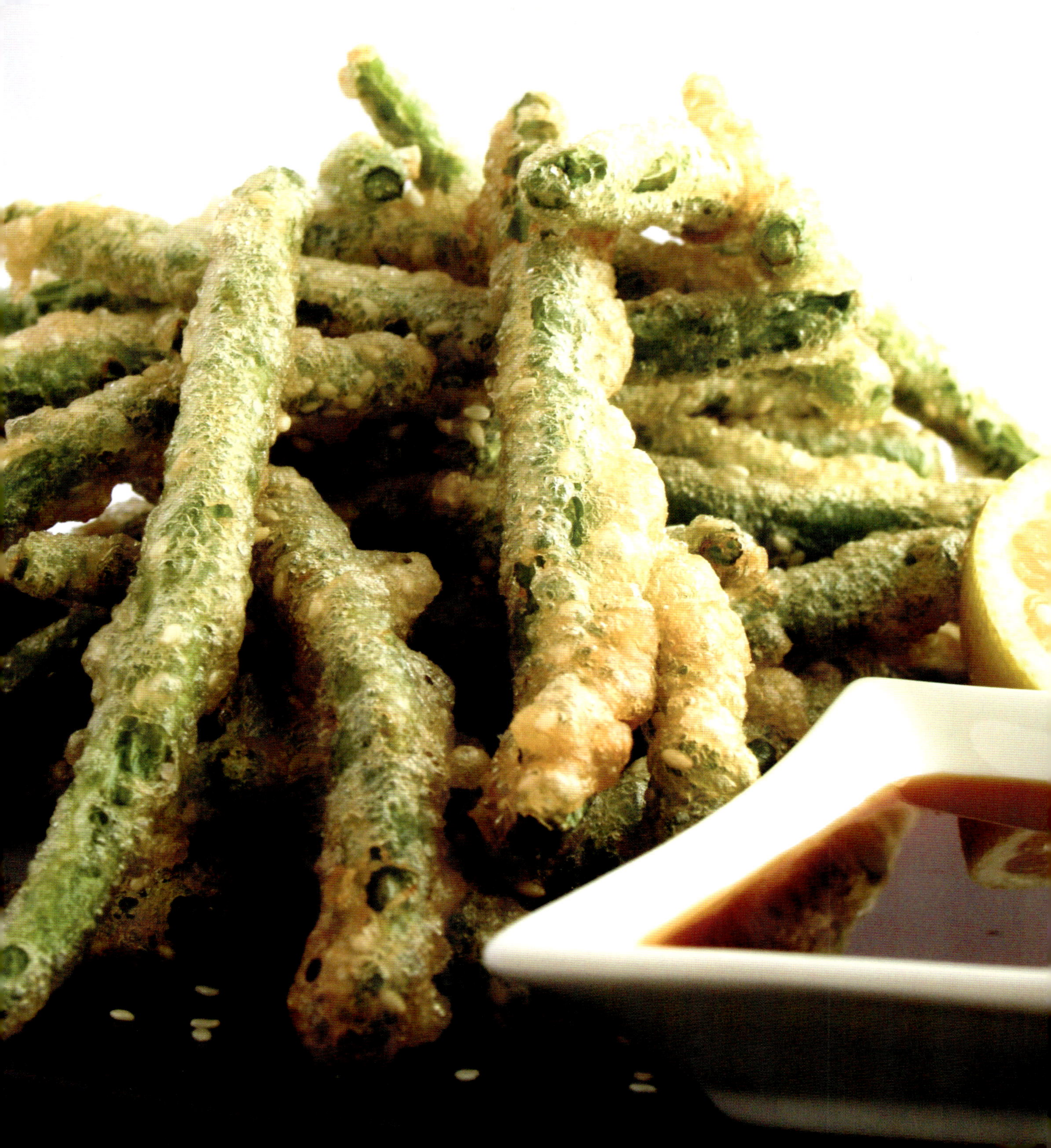

Braised Cabbage

Serves:	4
Preparation:	15-20 mins
Cooking:	25-35 mins

340ml beer (lager) – chef's tip: Steinlager Classic
225gm smoked bacon diced
1 large onion diced
1 medium head cabbage sliced
2 tablespoons caraway seeds
3 tablespoons wholegrain mustard
2 tablespoons sugar
Salt and cracked black pepper to season

Saucepan (large): cook the bacon over a low-medium heat. Add the onion, using the fat from the bacon to sweat it for 2-3 minutes until it is soft and translucent.

Add the beer, cabbage, caraway seeds, mustard and sugar and cover. Bring to the boil and immediately reduce to a low heat. Allow to simmer for about 30-35 minutes or until the cabbage is tender. Season with salt and black pepper.

Serving up

This cabbage is best served hot as a side dish for pork, chicken or with corned silverside (see recipe on page 112).

Carrots

Serves:	4
Preparation:	3-5 mins
Cooking:	15-20 mins

240ml beer (lager or draught) – chef's tip: Tui
3 large carrots
1 tablespoon butter
1½ teaspoons brown sugar
¼ teaspoon salt

Carrots are used so often as a side vegetable in New Zealand that it's easy to take them for granted. Here's a simple way to give them an extra boost of flavour.

Peel and cut the carrots into chunks.

Pot: over a low heat, melt the butter. Add the beer and carrots. Top up with water if needed to submerge the carrots. Cook until tender, stirring occasionally. Add the sugar and season with salt.

Simmer for 2 more minutes. Drain and serve while hot.

Mushroom & Barley

Serves:	4-5
Preparation:	15-20 mins
Cooking:	1¼-1½ hours

660ml beer (lager) – chef's tip: Export Gold
8 cups vegetable stock
4 tablespoons oil
2 medium onions diced
4 cloves garlic crushed
450gm flat mushrooms chopped
2 cups pearl barley
1½ teaspoons dried thyme
½ teaspoon salt
½ teaspoon ground black pepper
Parmesan cheese grated (garnish)
Cracked black pepper (garnish)

Pot (medium): mix the beer and stock and bring to the boil. Reduce heat and simmer.

Saucepan (large, deep): heat the oil over low-medium heat and saute the onions for 2 minutes. Add the garlic. Saute for 1 minute. Add the mushrooms and cook for 2-3 minutes. Add 4 cups of the beer/stock from the medium pot.

Add the barley, thyme, salt and pepper. Bring to the boil and simmer, covered, until the broth is absorbed by the barley. After this, you'll need to simmer the dish for 50-60 minutes or until the barley is tender, stirring occasionally and adding beer/stock a cup or two at a time. Stand for 2 minutes and serve.

Garnish with Parmesan cheese and cracked black pepper.

Asparagus Risotto

Serves:	4
Preparation:	5-10 mins
Cooking:	25-35 mins

250ml beer (lager) – chef's tip: Export Gold
4-5 cups chicken stock
1½ tablespoons oil
2 small shallots peeled and thinly sliced
2 cups Arborio rice
6 large asparagus cut into small slices
½ red capsicum finely diced
½ cup Parmesan cheese grated
Salt and cracked black pepper to season

Pot (medium): heat the chicken stock over medium heat and keep warm.

Saucepan (large, heavy base): heat the oil over low-medium heat and saute the shallots for about 2 minutes. Stir in the rice. Stir continuously for 2 minutes. Add the beer, stirring until it is fully absorbed.

Add 1 cup of the stock at a time, stirring until each is absorbed. It should take about 5 minutes for each cup of liquid to be absorbed. Continue for about 25-30 minutes until the rice is tender.

Stir in the asparagus and red capsicum and cook for 3-5 minutes, allowing the asparagus to become tender but not too soft. Stir in the Parmesan cheese. Season with salt and cracked black pepper.

Taste and add more Parmesan cheese if you want extra flavour.

Ratatouille

Serves:	4 as a side dish
Preparation:	15-20 mins
Cooking:	20-30 mins

60ml beer (lager) – chef's tip: Steinlager Pure
2 tablespoons oil
1 medium onion diced
6 garlic cloves crushed
1 tablespoon tomato paste
½ cup chicken stock
1 large eggplant (about 450gm) diced
1 medium courgette cut into ½cm-1cm cubes
1 medium green capsicum diced
6 medium button mushrooms quartered
1 420gm tin tomatoes chopped and drained
5 sprigs flat-leaf parsley chopped
4 sprigs of fresh basil chopped
Salt and cracked black pepper to season

The key to a good ratatouille is buying the best ingredients you can find and preparing them well. Wash the vegetables. Dice the capsicum, onion and eggplant. Cut the courgette into ½cm-1cm cubes. Quarter the mushrooms.

Pot (large, deep): heat the oil over low-medium heat. Saute the onion until soft. Add the garlic and continue cooking for a few minutes. Add the tomato paste and stir to combine.

When the paste begins to darken and stick, add the beer and stock. Turn up the heat until the liquid begins to simmer, and keep stirring to release flavours off the bottom of the pot.

Add the eggplant, courgette, capsicum and mushrooms. Cook over a medium heat for 10-12 minutes, stirring regularly. At first, it will seem as though you have way too much eggplant. Do not worry as the eggplant will start to fall apart and its juices will help cook and flavour the other ingredients.

The courgette, capsicum and mushrooms should be tender but not mushy. Add the drained tomatoes and warm for 1-2 minutes.

Chop the sprigs of parsley and basil and stir them into the pot. Season with salt and cracked black pepper. Serve hot.

'Beer is the reason I get up every afternoon.'

- *Anonymous*

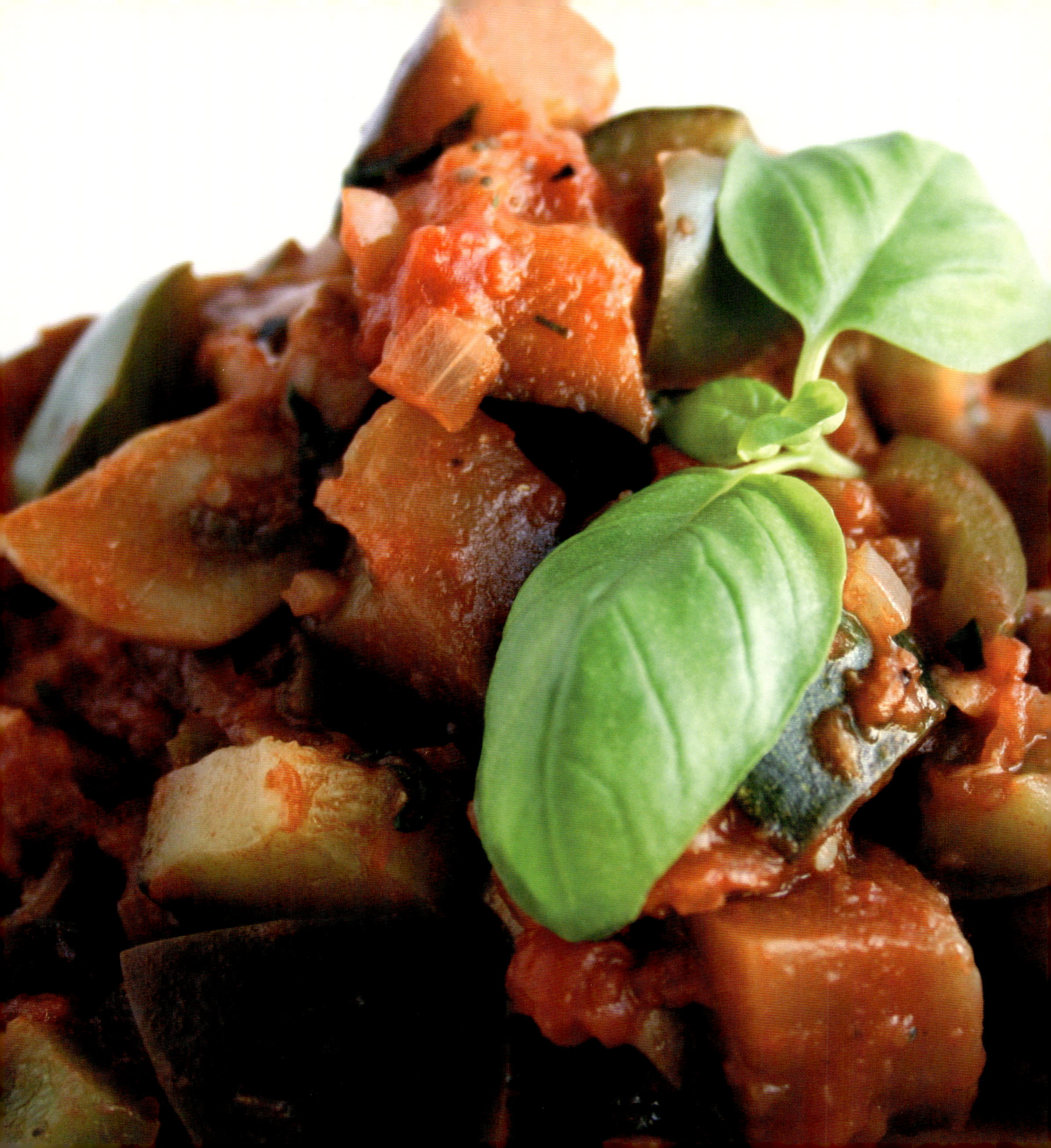

Beer Batter Onion Rings

Serves:	4
Preparation:	10-15 mins
Stand time:	10-15 mins
Cooking:	10-15 mins

330ml beer (lager or draught) – chef's tip: Lion Red
1½ cups all-purpose flour
½ teaspoon salt
¼ teaspoon white pepper
1 tablespoon oil
2 egg yolks
2 large onions thickly sliced
Vegetable oil for deep frying

Bowl 1: combine 1¼ cups of the flour, salt, pepper and oil and mix well. Add the beer and whisk to form a smooth batter. Add egg yolks and whisk in. Let the batter stand for 10-15 minutes.

Bowl 2: roll the onion rings in the remaining ¼ cup of flour and shake off any excess.

Deep fryer: heat your oil to 180°C. Dip the onion rings in the batter taking care to evenly coat them. Deep fry them in batches for 2-3 minutes or until golden brown.

Remove and drain on paper towels. Serve hot.

Beer Batter Vegetables

Serves:	4
Preparation:	10-15 mins
Stand time:	15 mins
Cooking:	12-15 mins

350ml beer (lager) – chef's tip: Export Gold
1 cup all-purpose flour
1 teaspoon baking powder
32gm packet onion soup mix – chef's tip: Maggi
2 eggs
Vegetable oil for deep frying

Vegetables

Halved button mushrooms, thin strips of carrot and courgette, and very thin slices of potato and kumara.

Bowl: sift the flour and baking powder into the bowl and add the onion soup mix and beer. Mix well and whisk until a smooth batter is formed. Whisk in the eggs.

Let the batter stand for 15 minutes before dipping the vegetables in the mix, taking care to evenly coat them.

Deep fryer: heat your oil to 170°C. Deep fry the vegetables in batches for 4-5 minutes or until golden brown.

Remove and drain on paper towels. Serve hot with a pinch of salt.

Kumara & Pineapple Salad

Serves:	8
Preparation:	25-30 mins
Refrigeration:	3 hours minimum
Cooking:	30 mins

350ml beer (dark) – chef's tip: Black Mac
450gm kumara peeled
1½ cups mayonnaise
½ teaspoon salt
¼ teaspoon white pepper
2 tablespoons brown sugar
1 tablespoon cider vinegar
1 tablespoon mild English mustard
4 spring onions thinly sliced
1 cup celery chopped
1 425gm tin pineapple chunks drained
120gm bacon bits, cooked (cold)

Pot (large): cut the kumara into 2cm cubes and place them in the pot. Add the beer and top up with water so the kumara are just covered. Bring to the boil and cook for 8-10 minutes or until they are just tender. Be careful not to let them overcook. Drain and cool. Refrigerate and chill for at least 2 hours.

Bowl (large): combine the mayonnaise, salt and pepper, brown sugar, vinegar and mustard until smooth. Stir in the spring onions and celery. Make sure the pineapple chunks are well-drained before cutting them in half and adding them to the bowl. Add the bacon pieces.

Finally, add the pieces of kumara, gently turning the salad so it is well mixed. Refrigerate and chill for at least 1 more hour.

Potato Salad

Serves:	8
Preparation:	15-20 mins
Stand time:	15 mins
Refrigeration:	1 hour minimum
Cooking:	10-12 mins

60ml beer (lager) – chef's tip: Mac's Gold
900gm potatoes peeled and cut into 1cm cubes
¾ cup sour cream
¾ cup mayonnaise
225gm bacon bits, cooked (cold)
¾ stick celery chopped
½ medium onion chopped
Salt and pepper to season

Pot (large): boil the potatoes for 10-12 minutes or until they just start to become tender. Drain and lay them on paper towels for 15 minutes to cool and dry. Refrigerate them for at least 1 hour.

Bowl (large): mix the beer, sour cream and mayonnaise in a large bowl. Add the bacon bits, celery and onion, folding the mixture over until the ingredients are evenly distributed. Finally, add the potato cubes and gently fold them into the mixture. Season with salt and pepper.

Refrigerate and serve cold.

Roasted Asparagus with Hollandaise Sauce

Serves:	4
Preparation:	5-10 mins
Cooking:	10-15 mins

120ml beer (lager) – chef's tip: Export Gold
170gm butter
1 bay leaf
5 black peppercorns
5 slices red onion
3 egg yolks
Juice from ½ lemon
450gm asparagus
1 tablespoon olive oil
Pinch of salt
Cracked black pepper

Pot 1 (small): for the sauce, melt the butter over low heat.

Pot 2 (small): boil the beer, bay leaf, black peppercorns and slices of red onion, uncovered, until the liquid reduces to about 2 tablespoons. Strain the bay leaf, peppercorns and red onion. Set aside.

Blender or food processor: blend the egg yolks. Add the contents of Pot 2 and the lemon juice. Slowly drizzle in the melted butter and process until the sauce thickens. Add more lemon juice to taste, if desired. Keep the sauce in a warm place.

Oven: preheat to 220°C. Trim the woody ends of the asparagus and spread the spears in a shallow roasting pan lined with non-stick baking paper. Drizzle the spears with olive oil, salt and cracked black pepper to season. Roast for about 10 minutes or until tender. Drizzle with the hollandaise sauce and top off with some more cracked black pepper.

Brussels Sprouts

Serves:	4
Preparation:	5 mins
Cooking:	15-20 mins

330ml-400ml beer (lager or draught) – chef's tip: Speight's Summit
400gm fresh Brussels sprouts
45gm butter
2 cloves garlic crushed
Salt and cracked black pepper to season
Fresh parsley chopped (optional)

Rinse and trim the sprouts.

Pot (large): cover the sprouts with beer and bring them to the boil over a medium-high heat. Immediately reduce the heat to low and simmer, covered, for about 15 minutes.

Do not cook the sprouts all the way through. Drain them and set aside to cool. Cut them in half lengthways.

Fry pan: melt the butter and add the garlic. Fry over a medium heat for 1 minute before adding the cut sprouts. Fry until golden brown.

Serving up

Serve the sprouts with a little of the remaining melted butter over the top, with salt and pepper to taste and some chopped parsley for garnish.

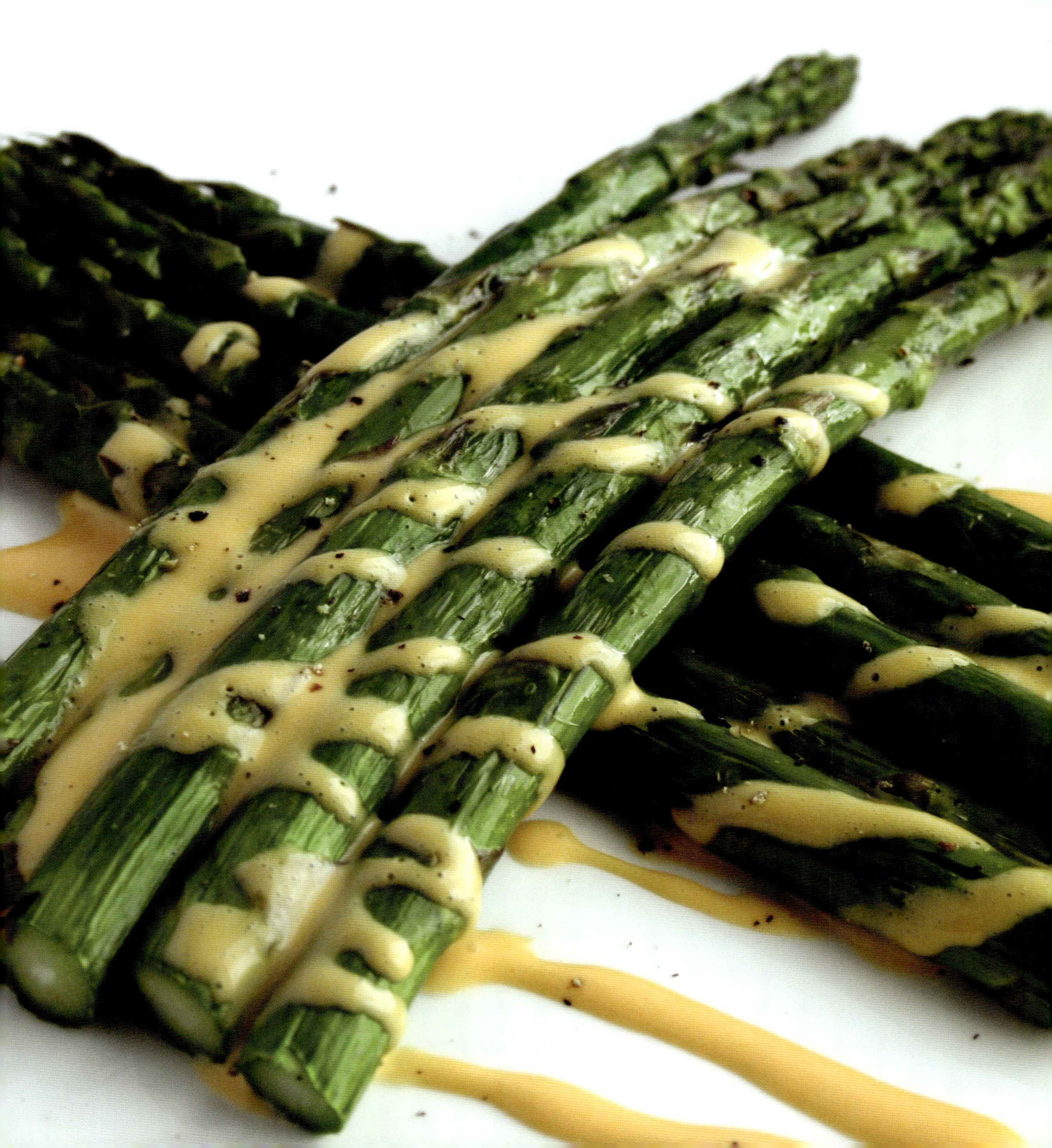

Potato Layer Cake

Serves:	4
Preparation:	20-25 mins
Cooking:	45-55 mins

125ml beer (lager or draught) – chef's tip: Tui
550gm potatoes peeled and thinly sliced
325gm kumara peeled and thinly sliced
30gm butter
2 tablespoons all-purpose flour
1 teaspoon Dijon mustard
100ml cream
100gm Cheddar cheese grated
2 teaspoons caraway seeds
2 teaspoons fresh rosemary finely chopped
Salt and pepper to season

Oven: preheat to 190°C.

Pot 1: place the sliced potatoes in sufficient water to cover them. Bring to the boil and maintain heat for 5 minutes. Remove the potatoes and lay them on paper towels. Gently pat them dry. Using the same pot, repeat the process with the kumara, boiling them for 4 minutes and then drying them.

Pot 2: melt the butter over low-medium heat. Add the flour and stir well for 1-2 minutes. Add the beer, and stir for 2 minutes, and then add mustard and cream. Mix well. Bring to the boil. Remove from the heat and stir in 75gm of the cheese, mixing well.

Baking dish (square, 22cm): grease the dish. Fill it with layers of potato, kumara and the sauce, sprinkling each layer with a small amount of caraway seeds and fresh rosemary and a little salt and pepper. Make sure the top layer is sauce and sprinkle with the remaining 25gm of cheese.

Oven: bake for 35-40 minutes until the top is golden.

Coleslaw

Serves:	12
Preparation:	15-20 mins
Refrigeration:	30 mins minimum

60ml beer (lager) – chef's tip: Mac's Gold
8 cups green cabbage shredded
1 cup of carrot grated
1½ tablespoons onion finely sliced
1 cup mayonnaise
Salt and cracked black pepper to season

Bowl 1 (large): combine the cabbage, carrot and onion in a large bowl.

Bowl 2: combine the beer and mayonnaise. When mixed well, pour them over the cabbage mix and toss. Season with salt and pepper.

Refrigerate the coleslaw for at least half an hour before serving.

Sauces and marinades

Sweet Mustard Sauce

Makes:	1 cup
Preparation:	5-10 mins

30ml beer (lager) – chef's tip: Export Gold
¾ cup mayonnaise
⅛ cup soft brown sugar
⅛ cup mild English mustard
⅛ cup liquid honey

Bowl: combine the ingredients in a bowl and mix well using an electric mixer until a smooth sauce is produced.

Serving up

This sauce goes well with beer-battered onion rings, chicken nuggets or a nice dipping sauce for fries.

Aioli

Makes:	1 cup
Preparation:	5-10 mins
Cooking:	35-40 mins

15ml beer (lager) – chef's tip: Steinlager Pure
1 large head of garlic
½ teaspoon olive oil
1 cup egg mayonnaise

Oven: preheat to 160°C.

Baking tray (non-stick): place the garlic on the baking tray and brush with olive oil. Bake for 35-40 mins or until soft. Remove and stand to cool.

Bowl (small): when the garlic is cool, squeeze the cloves from the skin and mash with a wooden spoon.

Bowl (medium): combine the beer and egg mayonnaise. Add the garlic. Mix well.

Satay Sauce

Makes:	about 1 cup
Preparation:	5-10 mins
Cooking:	5-10 mins

125ml beer (lager) – chef's tip: Mac's Gold
½ cup smooth peanut butter
½ cup sugar
3 tablespoons light soy sauce
1 clove garlic crushed
½ teaspoon red pepper flakes
¼ teaspoon sesame oil

Saucepan: combine the ingredients in the saucepan, stirring with a wooden spoon. Heat over a low-medium heat, stirring regularly to ensure the sauce is smooth and warmed through.

The sauce will continue to thicken when removed from the heat.

Serving up

This sauce is best with chicken or on vegetables.

Tangy Tomato Sauce

Makes:	2 cups
Preparation:	5-10 mins
Cooking:	35-40 mins

350ml beer (lager or draught) – chef's tip: Tui
1½ cups tomato sauce
¾ medium onion diced
½ cup malt vinegar
1½ tablespoons prepared mustard
1½ tablespoons Worcestershire sauce
½ teaspoon hot pepper sauce – chef's tip: Kaitaia Fire
1 teaspoon salt

Saucepan: combine all the ingredients and heat over a medium-high heat. When the sauce comes to the boil, immediately reduce heat and simmer, uncovered, for 30-35 minutes.

Serving up

Best served warm at your barbecue.

Cocktail Sauce

Serves:	4
Preparation:	5-10 mins

1 tablespoon beer (lager) – chef's tip: Export Gold
200gm mayonnaise
2 tablespoons tomato sauce
1 teaspoon Worcestershire sauce
1 teaspoon lemon juice or to taste
Salt to season
Drop of hot pepper sauce (optional) – chef's tip: Kaitaia Fire

Bowl (small): combine all the ingredients in a small bowl and mix well.

Chill.

Serving up

This makes a good dipping sauce for cold seafood such as prawns or to make a prawn cocktail.

Tartare Sauce

Makes:	1 cup
Preparation:	15-20 mins

235ml beer (lager) – chef's tip: Mac's Gold
1 tablespoon oil
2 cloves garlic crushed
1 shallot minced
2 teaspoons sweet chilli sauce
1 cup mayonnaise
2 tablespoons sweet gerkins finely diced
1 teaspoon fresh parsley finely chopped
Salt and pepper to season

Saucepan: heat the oil over a medium heat and sweat the garlic and shallot for about 3 minutes until they are soft. Add the beer and cook until the mixture is reduced to about $\frac{1}{4}$ cup.

Remove the saucepan from the heat and allow the mixture to cool.

Bowl: combine the sweet chilli, mayonnaise, gerkins and parsley. Add the beer reduction and mix well. Season with salt and pepper.

Serving up

This is an excellent sauce to serve with fish (especially beer battered fish).

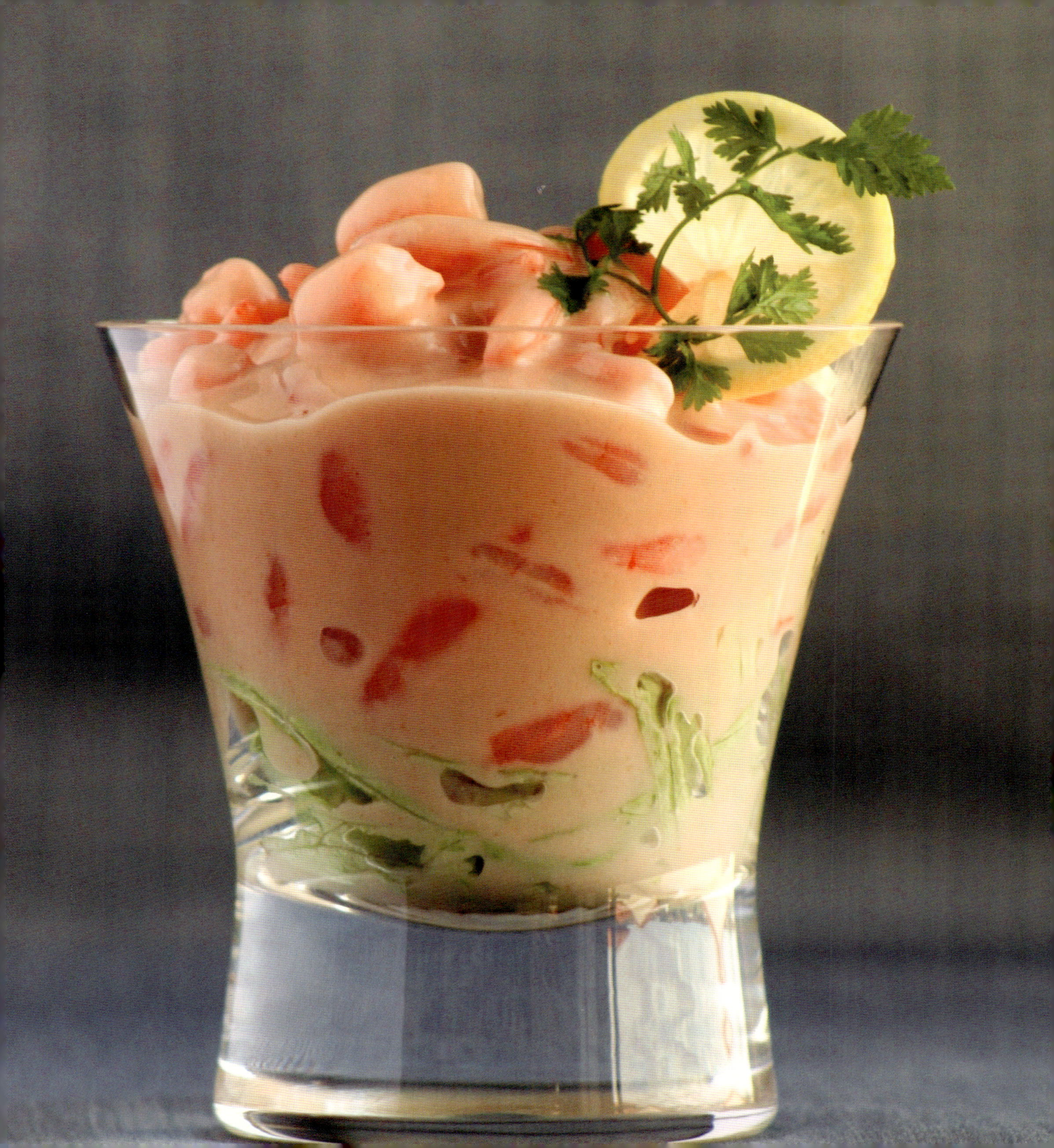

Blue Cheese Sauce

Makes:	about 1½ cups
Preparation:	10-15 mins
Cooking:	15-25 mins

120ml beer (lager) – chef's tip: Mac's Gold
2 tablespoons oil
1 teaspoon butter
2 cups onion diced
2 teaspoons brown sugar
½ teaspoon dried thyme
1 teaspoon lemon zest
1 tablespoon chives finely chopped
1 tablespoon red capsicum finely diced
1 cup creamy blue cheese crumbled – chef's tip: Mainland Special Reserve Creamy Blue

Saucepan: gently heat the oil and butter over a low heat and add the onions. Stir and cover for 10-15 minutes or until the onions are soft and translucent. Add the brown sugar, stir and cover for 5-7 minutes until the onions are caramelised.

Pour in the beer and add the thyme, lemon zest, chives and capsicum. Heat over low-medium heat. Add the crumbled cheese and stir until the mixture becomes a smooth sauce.

Serving up

Serve warm. This sauce works a treat with steak.

Bearnaise Sauce

Makes:	about 1 cup
Preparation:	5-10 mins
Cooking:	10-15 mins

125ml beer (lager) – chef's tip: Export Gold
170gm butter
5 black peppercorns
1 bay leaf
5 slices red onion
3 egg yolks
Juice of ½ lemon and more to taste
2½ teaspoons fresh tarragon chopped

Pot 1: melt the butter over low heat.

Pot 2: boil the beer, peppercorns, bay leaf and red onion, uncovered, until the liquid reduces to about 2 tablespoons. Strain the peppercorns, bay leaf and red onion and discard.

Blender or food processor: blend the egg yolks. Add the contents of Pot 2 and the lemon juice. Slowly drizzle in the melted butter and process until the sauce thickens. Add more lemon juice to taste, if desired. Stir in the fresh tarragon. Keep the sauce in a warm place until needed.

Serving up

This sauce is a good match for steaks and fish.

Sweet Bacon Sauce

Makes:	about 1½ cups
Preparation:	10-15 mins
Cooking:	20-35 mins

240ml beer (draught) – chef's tip: Speight's Gold Medal Ale
450gm bacon
½ cup cider vinegar
½ medium onion chopped
2 teaspoons mustard powder
1 cup brown sugar
2½ tablespoons all-purpose flour

Fry pan (large): fry the bacon until well done and almost crisp. Remove from the pan and stand to cool.

Leave the bacon grease in the pan and add the vinegar, onion, mustard powder and sugar. Heat over medium heat.

Bowl: combine the beer and flour. Add this mix to the fry pan and continue to stir over medium heat. After 5-7 minutes, the mixture should thicken.

Chop the bacon into pieces and add to the sauce. Allow to cool.

Serving up

This sauce works well over fresh spinach salad or warm chicken salad.

Garlic & Herb Butter

Makes:	1½ cups
Preparation:	15-20 mins
Stand time:	1 hour

30ml beer (lager or draught) – chef's tip: Export Lager
230gm butter softened
¼ teaspoon salt
2 tablespoons chives finely chopped
1 spring onion finely chopped
1 teaspoon dried thyme
1 teaspoon dried basil
1 teaspoon dried marjoram
1 clove garlic crushed
¼ teaspoon ground black pepper

Bowl: cream the butter with the salt and beer in the bowl.

Blend in the other ingredients in stages, mixing well.

Cover and leave to stand at room temperature for 1 hour.

Serving up

This butter can be used in many ways – with baked fish, on steak or to make garlic bread.

Onion Gravy

Serves:	4-6
Preparation:	20-30 mins
Cooking:	1¼-1½ hours

500ml beer (draught) – chef's tip: Lion Red
2 tablespoons oil
25gm butter
700gm onions thinly sliced
1 tablespoon caster sugar
1 tablespoon all-purpose flour
2½ cups beef stock
½ star anise
2 bay leaves
Salt and cracked black pepper to season

Saucepan (large, heavy base): heat the oil and butter over low-medium heat. Add the onions, sweating them for about 5 minutes. Reduce the heat to low heat. Add the sugar and cook for about 45-50 minutes, stirring often. The onions will soften and become caramelised.

Add the flour, stir and cook for 1 minute. Add the beer, stock, star anise and bay leaves and stir. Turn up the heat to high and boil, uncovered, for about 18-20 minutes until the gravy reduces to a glossy sauce.

Remove the bay leaves and star anise. Season with salt and pepper.

Serving up

This gravy can turn an otherwise-ordinary sausages and mash meal into a feast!

Pork Basting Sauce

Makes:	2¾ cups
Preparation:	5 mins

165ml beer (lager) – chef's tip: Monteith's Golden
½ cup apple sauce
¼ cup maple syrup
Salt and pepper to season

Bowl: combine the beer, apple sauce and maple syrup, mixing well. Season with salt and pepper.

This provides a sweet sauce for basting roast pork or pork chops.

Onion Gravy served over Sausages & Mash (see recipe on page 124) ▶

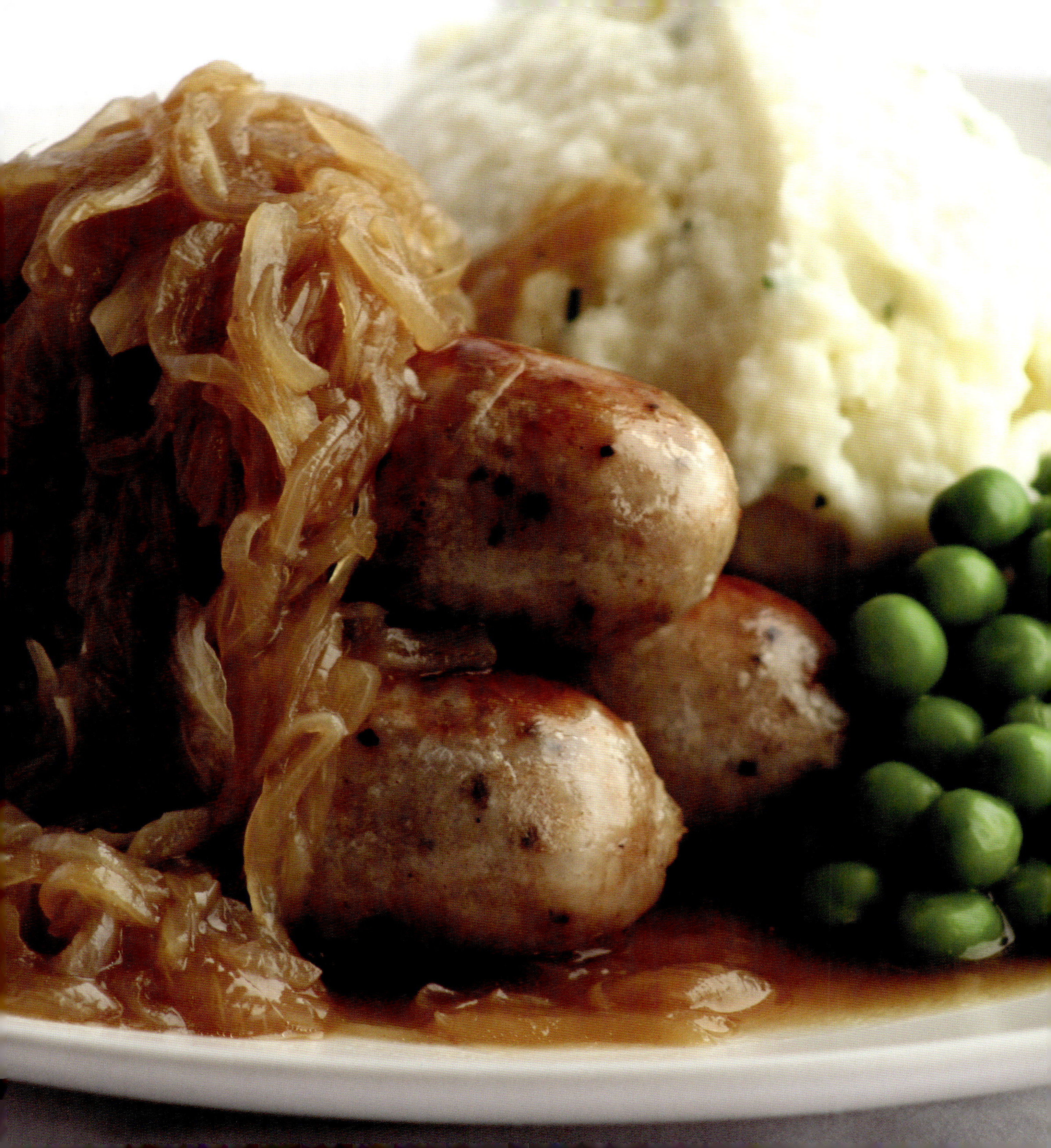

Soy & Ginger Steak Marinade

Enough for: 4 steaks
Preparation: 5-10 mins
Refrigeration: 2 hours minimum

120ml beer (lager) – chef's tip: Export Gold
½ cup soy sauce
¼ cup maple syrup
4 cloves garlic sliced
1 tablespoon fresh ginger grated
1 teaspoon mustard powder
½ teaspoon sesame oil

Bowl: combine all ingredients and mix well.

Baking dish (glass): lay your steaks flat in the dish. Pour the marinade over the steaks. Cover with plastic wrap and refrigerate for at least 2 hours to achieve the maximum flavour.

Remove steaks from marinade and cook.

Lime Steak Marinade

Enough for: 4-6 steaks
Preparation: 5-10 mins
Refrigeration: 2 hours minimum

350ml beer (lager) – chef's tip: Monteith's Golden
½ cup brown sugar
6 tablespoons fresh lime juice
4 cloves garlic sliced
3 tablespoons Worcestershire sauce
4 tablespoons olive oil
3 tablespoons whole grain mustard

Bowl: combine all ingredients and whisk until thoroughly mixed.

Baking dish (glass): lay your steaks flat in the dish. Pour the marinade over the steaks. Cover with plastic wrap and refrigerate for at least 2 hours to achieve the maximum flavour.

Remove steaks from marinade and cook.

Herb Steak Marinade

Enough for:	4-6 steaks
Preparation:	10-15 mins
Refrigeration:	2 hours minimum

250ml beer (lager) – chef's tip: Steinlager Pure
¼ cup fresh basil finely chopped
2 tablespoons fresh tarragon finely chopped
1 tablespoon fresh thyme finely chopped
¼ cup shallots chopped
3 cloves garlic crushed
1 teaspoon coarsely cracked black pepper
½ teaspoon salt
½ cup oil

Blender or food processor: combine all the ingredients except the oil and process until fully blended. While the motor is running, slowly drizzle in the oil.

Baking dish (glass): lay your steaks flat in a the dish. Pour the marinade over the steaks. Cover with plastic wrap and refrigerate for at least 2 hours to achieve the maximum flavour.

Remove steaks from marinade and stand at room temperature for about 5 minutes. Pat dry and cook.

Salmon Marinade

Enough for:	4-6 fillets
Preparation:	10-15 mins
Refrigeration:	1 hour maximum

240ml beer (lager) – chef's tip: Steinlager Pure
1 cup light soy sauce
6 tablespoons fresh lime juice
¼ cup olive oil
2 tablespoons onion finely chopped
2 tablespoons brown sugar
2 tablespoons white vinegar
1 teaspoon mustard powder
½ teaspoon ground ginger
½ teaspoon ground cinnamon

Blender or food processor: combine all the ingredients and process until mixed well.

Baking dish (glass): lay the fish flat in the dish and marinate the fish for no longer than 1 hour before cooking as the acid from the lime will start to cook the fish.

Remove the fish from the marinade and cook immediately.

The marinade also works well with trout and other non-white fish.

Lamb Marinade

Enough for:	1 roast leg
Preparation:	5-10 mins
Refrigeration:	2 hours minimum

240ml beer (lager) – chef's tip: Mac's Gold
4 tablespoons olive oil
2 tablespoons fresh rosemary leaves
3 cloves garlic sliced
Peel of 1 lemon, using vegetable peeler to scrape thin strips and cut in half

This marinade works particularly well with roasting legs and lamb chops for the grill.

Bowl: combine all ingredients and mix well.

Baking dish (glass): lay your lamb flat in the dish. Pour the marinade over the meat, cover with plastic wrap and refrigerate for at least 2 hours to achieve the maximum flavour. Turn the meat in the marinade regularly.

Remove the lamb and pat dry with paper towel before cooking

Venison Marinade

Enough for:	4-6 steaks
Preparation:	10-15 mins
Refrigeration:	2 hours minimum

350ml beer (dark) – chef's tip: Black Mac
125ml Worcestershire sauce
2 cloves garlic sliced
1½ cups all-purpose flour
1 tablespoon onion salt
Oil for frying

This marinade works in two stages.

Baking dish (glass): pour the beer, Worcestershire sauce and sliced garlic over the venison laid flat in a baking dish. Cover with plastic wrap and refrigerate for at least 2 hours.

Bowl: combine the flour and onion salt and mix well. When the venison has been removed from the beer and Worcestershire sauce, pat it dry and roll it in the flour mix. Shake off excess flour.

Fry pan (heavy): fry the venison in a hot pan with a small amount of oil.

Serving up

Venison goes particularly well with grilled chorizo sausage.

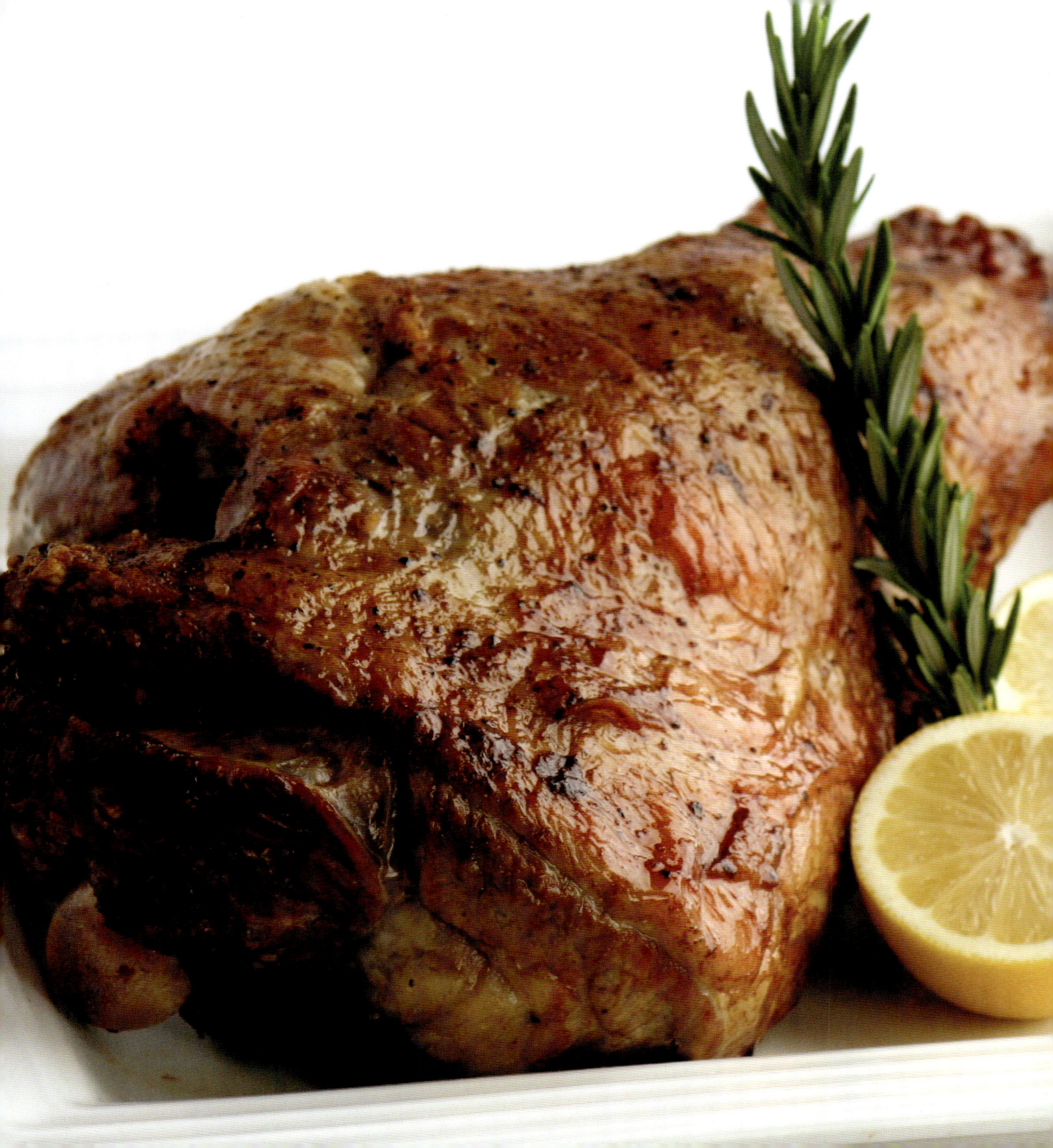

Pizza & Pasta Sauce

Makes:	2 cups
Preparation:	10-15 mins
Cooking:	15-20 mins

60ml beer (lager) – chef's tip: Export Gold
2 tablespoons dried basil
¼ cup fresh basil sliced
1 teaspoon dried oregano
2 teaspoons oil
½ cup onion grated
4 cloves garlic crushed
3 cups fresh tomatoes chopped
1 tablespoon tomato paste
1 teaspoon brown sugar (plus more to taste, if desired)

This sauce is extremely versatile – it can be used with pasta dishes and on your pizza bases.

Bowl (small): combine the fresh basil, dried basil and oregano and pour in the beer. Stir and leave to sit for 10 minutes.

Saucepan (large, deep): heat the oil over medium-high heat. Sweat the onions with the garlic, stirring constantly, for 5 minutes. Add the tomatoes, tomato paste and sugar. Stir well.

Add the basil/oregano/beer mix and stir in. Cover and cook for 15 minutes, stirring occasionally. Taste the sauce and add another teaspoon of brown sugar if you prefer your sauce sweeter.

Blender or food processor: remove the sauce from the heat and transfer the contents to a blender or food processor. Puree.

Container (sealed): this sauce keeps well in the refrigerator so can be used over several days. Store in a well-sealed container.

'Beer makes you feel the way you ought to feel without beer.'

- Henry Lawson

Something fishy

Mussels with Salsa

Serves:	2
Preparation:	35-50 mins
Cooking:	10-15 mins

250ml beer (lager or draught) – chef's tip: Steinlager Pure
1.25kg green-lipped mussels scrubbed and debearded
1 tablespoon oil
1 clove garlic crushed
2 cups salsa – see recipe on page 14

Garnish

Lemon wedges

First, throw away any mussels with broken shells.

Pot (large, deep): heat the oil in a large pot over low-medium heat. Add the garlic and sweat for 1-2 minutes.

Add the mussels, followed by the beer. Crank up the heat to high, mix well and cover. As the heat builds, the steam should open the shells and cook the mussels. Keep covered and shake the pan occasionally while this happens.

When the mussel shells have opened (discard any that have not opened) remove the mussels from the pot and place in serving bowls.

Add the salsa to the liquid remaining in the pot and stir to warm through. Spoon the salsa over the mussels, adding some of the broth. Garnish with lemon wedges.

Chorizo Mussels

Serves:	3
Preparation:	15-25 mins
Cooking:	10-15 mins

330ml beer (lager) – chef's tip: Steinlager Pure
1 tablespoon oil
200gm chorizo sausage cut into 1cm cubes
50gm shallots sliced
3 cloves garlic crushed
1 fresh red chilli finely sliced
1.75kg green-lipped mussels scrubbed and debearded

Garnish

4 tablespoons fresh parsley finely chopped
Lemon wedges

First, throw away any mussels with broken shells.

Pot (large, deep): heat the oil over low-medium heat. Add the chorizo sausage and shallots and saute for 1-2 minutes. Add the garlic and chilli and saute until the sausage, garlic and shallots start to colour.

Add the mussels, followed by the beer. Crank up the heat to high, mix well and cover. As the heat builds, the steam should open the shells and cook the mussels. Keep covered and shake the pan occasionally while this happens.

When the mussel shells have opened (discard any that have not opened) transfer them to serving bowls. Using a slotted spoon, place the chorizo mix over the mussels adding some of the broth.

Garnish with chopped parsley and wedges of fresh lemon.

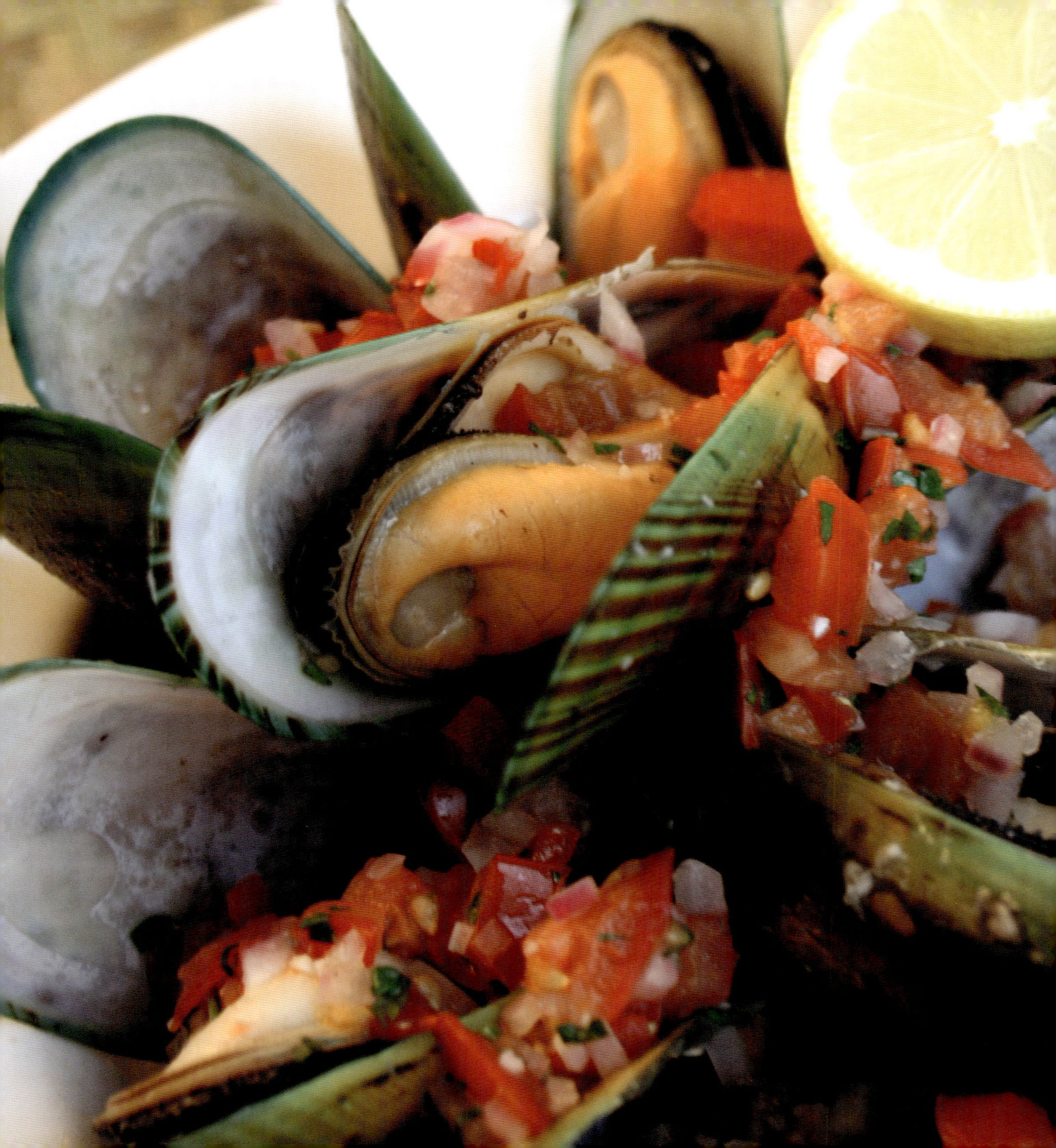

Oysters

Serves:	4
Preparation:	10-15 mins
Cooking:	10-15 mins

125ml beer (lager or draught) – chef's tip: Steinlager Pure
1 cup self-raising flour
Pinch of salt
½ cup cold water
2 dozen oysters
¼ cup fresh dill chopped
Extra flour for coating oysters
Enough vegetable oil for deep frying

Bowl: sift the flour and salt into the bowl. Make a well and pour in the beer and water. Mix well to form a smooth batter.

Plastic bag: drain the oysters and place them in the bag. Add the dill and just enough flour to coat the oysters. Gently shake the bag, rotating the contents so the oysters become lightly coated with flour. Shake off excess flour.

Deep fryer: preheat the oil to 180°C. Dip each oyster into the batter and deep fry them in batches for 2-4 minutes or until they rise to the surface and are crisp and golden. Drain the oysters on paper towels.

Serving up

Serve with your favourite dipping sauces. Plain lemon juice is good too.

Oyster & Watercress Risotto

Serves:	4
Preparation:	10-15 mins
Cooking:	35-50 mins

250ml beer (dark) – chef's tip: Black Mac
1.25 litres hot chicken stock
2 tablespoons oil
1 red onion diced
2 cloves garlic crushed
1 cup mushrooms sliced
2 cups Arborio rice
2 dozen oysters
Cracked black pepper to season
Juice of 1 lemon and zest from ½ lemon
½ cup fresh watercress chopped

Pot: heat the chicken stock over a medium heat and keep hot.

Saucepan (large, heavy based): heat the oil over a low-medium heat. Add the onion and saute for 3 minutes. Add the garlic and cook for 2 minutes, stirring. Add the mushrooms and heat for 2 minutes. Add the rice and stir for 2 minutes. Add the beer and half a cup of stock. Stir constantly over medium heat until the liquid has almost been absorbed.

Add the remaining hot chicken stock to the risotto a cup at a time, stirring until the liquid is absorbed each time. Stir regularly and add stock for 25-30 minutes until the rice is soft.

Stir in the oysters, pepper, lemon juice and lemon zest, and cook for 1-2 minutes. Remove from the heat and stir in the watercress just before serving.

Steamed Crayfish

Serves:	2
Preparation:	5 mins
Cooking:	10-15 mins

330ml beer (lager) – chef's tip: Mac's Gold or Steinlager Pure
2 cooked crayfish tails (thawed if frozen) out of the shell or split lengthways
Warm melted butter or cocktail sauce – see recipe on page 66

Pot (large): heat the beer over medium-high heat, bringing it to the boil.

Steamer: place the crayfish tails in a steamer basket or colander and sit it on top of the pot. Cover to trap in the steam.

Reduce the heat to low and simmer for about 8-10 minutes or until the crayfish is heated through.

Serving up

Serve with melted butter or cocktail sauce (see recipe on page 66).

Poached Salmon

Serves:	4
Preparation:	5-10 mins
Cooking:	12-15 mins

330ml beer (lager) – chef's tip: Steinlager Pure
4 salmon fillets
1 medium onion chopped
1 teaspoon salt
¼ teaspoon white pepper
2 tablespoons fresh dill
2 slices fresh lemon

This method of poaching salmon is healthy and provides the fish with a delicate texture and taste.

Saucepan (large, deep): combine all the ingredients, except the fish, and raise the fluid level by adding cold water until there is sufficient liquid to just cover the fillets.

Mix well. Bring to the boil over medium-high heat. Reduce the heat. Add the fish, laying the fillets in a single layer across the pan, skin side down. Simmer on low heat, covered, for about 12-15 minutes or until the fish is cooked and easily flakes. Carefully remove the fish, leaving the pieces of onion, dill and lemon in the pan.

Serving up

Try serving the fish over steamed vegetables or roasted asparagus, topped with hollandaise sauce (see recipe on page 60).

Garlic Prawns

Serves:	4
Preparation:	5-10 mins
Cooking:	5-10 mins

125ml beer (lager) – chef's tip: Export Gold
4 tablespoons butter
4 cloves garlic crushed
1 teaspoon dried oregano
1 teaspoon dried basil
1 teaspoon dried thyme
½ teaspoon crushed red chilli flakes
900gm raw prawns peeled and deveined
Fresh coriander chopped (optional)
¼ red capsicum finely diced (optional)

Saucepan (large, deep): slightly warm the butter over a medium heat. Add the garlic, oregano, basil, thyme and red chilli flakes. Saute until the garlic is lightly browned and the butter is bubbling.

Add the prawns and increase the heat to medium-high, gently stirring the prawns until they all turn pink.

Pour in the beer and simmer, uncovered, for 1-2 minutes.

Serving up

These prawns are particularly tasty if served with your choice of rice and topped with some fresh chopped coriander and finely diced red capsicum.

Prawns with Yoghurt Dip

Serves:	2-4
Preparation:	15-20 mins
Cooking:	10 mins

330ml beer (lager) – chef's tip: Export Gold
½ cup plain yoghurt
1½ tablespoons mayonnaise
1½ tablespoons sweet chilli sauce
¼ teaspoon Worcestershire sauce
½ teaspoon lemon juice
1 teaspoon garlic powder
4 peppercorns
1 bay leaf
1 whole clove
2 dozen raw prawns peeled and deveined

Bowl: to make the yoghurt dip, combine the yoghurt, mayonnaise, sweet chilli sauce, Worcestershire sauce and lemon juice. Mix well. Refrigerate and chill.

Saucepan (large): over medium-high heat, combine the beer, garlic powder, peppercorns, bay leaf and clove. Boil for 4-5 minutes.

Remove from the heat and add the prawns. Stand, covered, for 3-5 minutes but turning the prawns over after 2-3 minutes. They will turn pink.

Container: drain the prawns and allow them to cool. Transfer them to a container. Chill in the refrigerator.

Serving up

Offer the prawns with the yoghurt dip on the side.

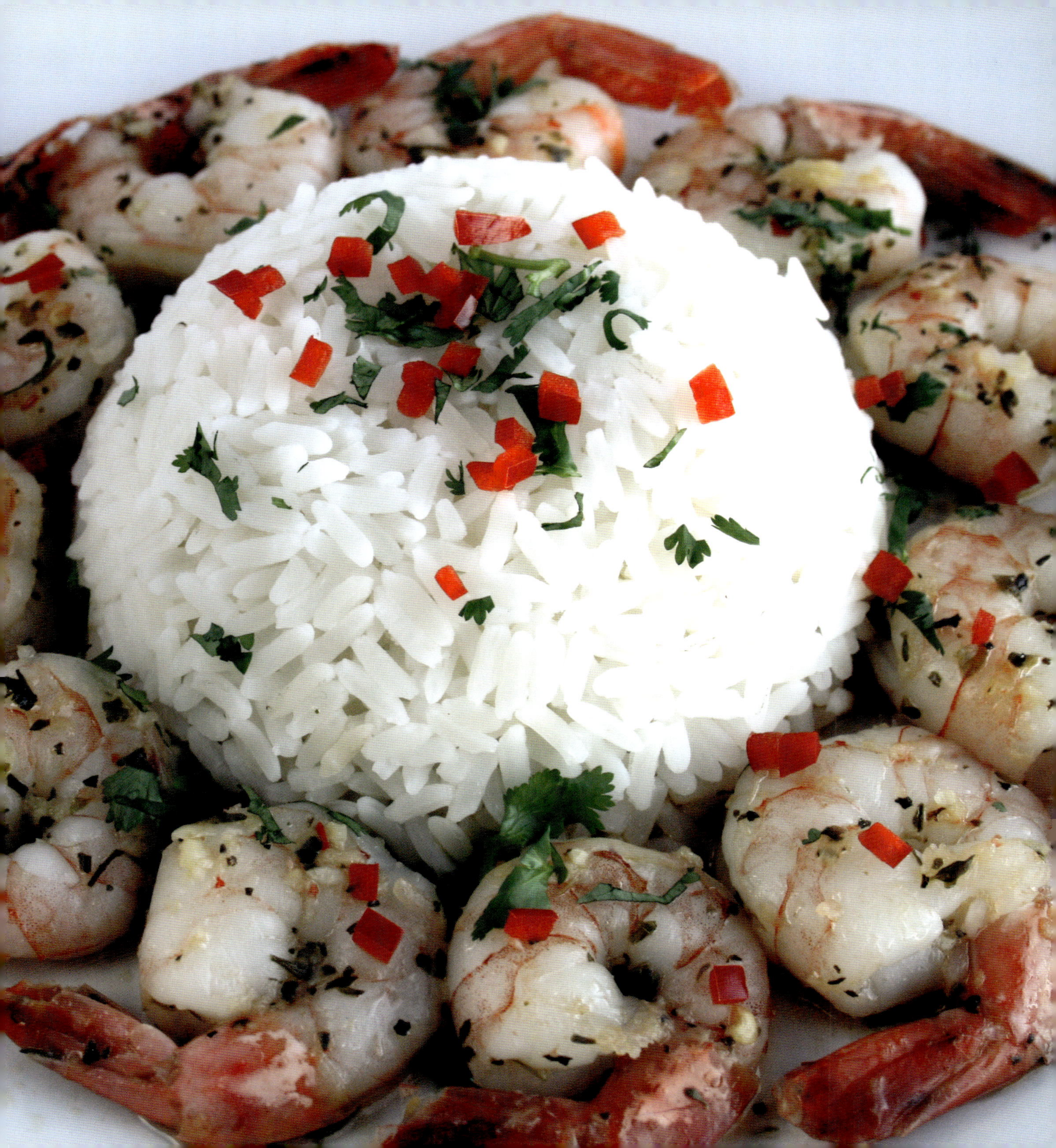

Almond-crusted Trout Fillets

Serves:	4
Preparation:	20-25 mins
Cooking:	15-20 mins

250ml beer (lager) – chef's tip: Export Gold
½ cup seasoned dried bread crumbs
1 cup toasted almonds
4 large trout fillets (or salmon)
Juice of 2 lemons
Salt and pepper
1 egg
1 tablespoon of beer (lager)
4 tablespoons all-purpose flour
2 tablespoons oil
2 teaspoons sugar

Blender or food processor: process half the bread crumbs with the almonds. Transfer to Bowl 1.

Bowl 1: combine with the remaining bread crumbs.

Bowl 2: sit the fish fillets in the juice of 1 lemon and season with salt and pepper. Leave for 10 minutes.

Oven: preheat to 200°C.

Bowl 3: beat the egg with 1 tablespoon of lager.

Bowl 4: line the bowl with flour.

Dredge the fillets through the flour. Shake off any excess. Then dip them in the egg bowl and gently roll in the bowl of bread crumbs. Press until each fillet is evenly coated.

Fry pan (large): heat the oil over medium heat. Fry the fish, lightly browning it on all sides. This should take 1-2 minutes each side.

Baking dish: place the fish in a baking dish and bake for about 5-7 minutes or until it is cooked to your liking.

Saucepan: combine the lager, the juice of 1 lemon and 2 teaspoons of sugar in the pan. Boil until the liquid reduces to about a third of its original volume.

Drizzle this lager glaze over the fish and serve.

Steamed Pipis or Cockles with Bacon

Serves:	4
Preparation:	15-20 mins
Cooking:	15-20 mins

240ml beer (lager) – chef's tip: Mac's Gold
2 teaspoons oil
225gm bacon diced
1 small onion diced
2 cloves garlic chopped
1.5kg pipis or cockles

Garnish

Fresh parsley chopped
Lemon wedges

Pot (deep): heat 2 teaspoons of oil over medium heat and fry the bacon and onion for 3-4 minutes. Add the garlic and cook for 2-3 minutes or until the bacon starts to brown and the onion and garlic are tender.

Add the shellfish to the pot followed by the beer. Stir, cover and bring to the boil. Steam the shellfish for 3-5 minutes or until they are open. Discard any shellfish that have not opened.

Serving up

Transfer the shellfish to bowls. Using a slotted spoon, drain the bacon, garlic and onion from the pot and distribute over the shellfish. Garnish with chopped parsley and lemon wedges.

Beer Batter Fish

Makes:	coats 4 fish fillets
Preparation:	5-10 mins

330ml beer (lager or draught) – chef's tip: Tui
1¼ cups all-purpose flour
1 teaspoon paprika
Pinch salt
Flour for dusting

This is a simple but effective batter that works well with fish.

Bowl 1: sift the flour, paprika and salt into the bowl and make a well. Pour in the beer and whisk until a smooth batter has formed. Allow to stand for 1 minute before using.

Bowl 2: sift the dusting flour into a bowl and gently roll the fish through it, shaking off any excess flour. Dip the fish into the batter in Bowl 1 and deep fry until golden brown.

Fish in Beer & Vodka Batter

Serves:	4
Preparation:	15-20 mins
Cooking:	30-45 mins

240ml beer (lager or draught) – chef's tip: Mac's Gold
Vegetable oil for deep frying
2 cups all-purpose flour plus extra for dusting
¾ teaspoon baking powder
½ teaspoon salt
240ml vodka
Salt and white pepper to season
Fresh lemons (optional)

Fish – your choice. This batter is sufficient to coat 700gm-800gm of fish fillets.

Cut the fish fillets into the sizes you want to serve.

Deep fryer: to prepare, you will need oil to a depth of 4-5cm. Set the temperature to 180°C. If using a stove top fryer, heat the oil until a cube of bread crisps easily and quickly.

Bowl: to make the batter, combine the 2 cups of all-purpose flour, the baking powder and salt.

Slowly add the vodka and beer, stirring it into the dry ingredients to make the batter. The beer should create a foam – this is what makes this type of batter fluffier than others.

Be careful not to make this batter too far ahead of cooking as it can go flat.

Plate: season the fish with salt and pepper. Dust with a small amount of the flour and shake off the excess.

Deep fryer: dip each fillet of fish into the batter, coating it completely, and carefully lower into the oil. When the fillets start to turn golden brown underneath, turn them and brown their other sides.

Remove the cooked fillets from the oil, drain and serve.

Serving up

Offer plenty of fresh lemon wedges on the side. A good way to increase the juice from the lemon is to roll it on a firm surface, under the pressure of your hand, before cutting it into wedges.

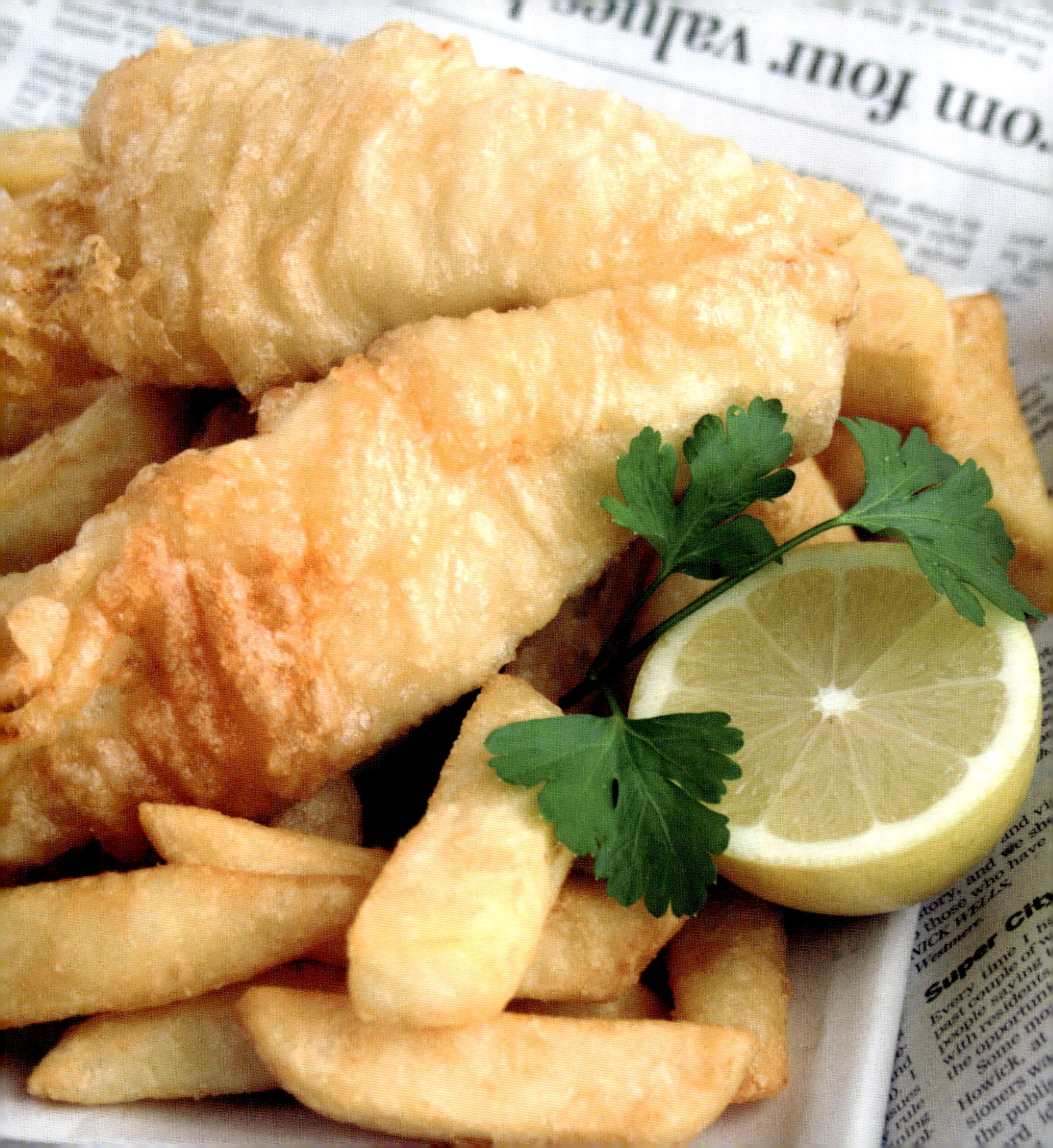

Teriyaki Fish

Serves:	4
Preparation:	5-10 mins
Stand time:	1 hour
Refrigeration:	2 hours
Cooking:	5-10 mins

80ml beer (dark) – chef's tip: Black Mac
¼ cup honey warmed
3 tablespoons tamari or light soy sauce
2 tablespoons oil
1 tablespoon sugar
1 tablespoon sesame oil
2 cloves garlic crushed
½ teaspoon fresh ginger chopped
Pinch of ground black pepper
6 fish fillets – chef's tip: tuna or swordfish

This recipe works well with firm-fleshed fish such as tuna or swordfish.

Bowl (large): take all the ingredients except the fish and combine them. Whisk to form a marinade. Leave to stand at room temperature for 1 hour.

Baking dish (glass): lay the fish flat and generously brush the fish with the marinade. Cover with plastic wrap and refrigerate for 2 hours.

Fry pan or grill pan: fry the fish in a shallow pan, or chargrill it, basting with more marinade to your taste as it cooks.

Asian-style Salmon

Serves:	4
Preparation:	20-25 mins
Cooking:	20-25 mins

175ml beer (lager) – chef's tip: Export Gold
2 tablespoons fresh ginger grated
2 cloves garlic crushed
2 tablespoons spring onion bulbs thinly sliced
1 tablespoon chives chopped
2 tablespoons fresh coriander finely chopped
1 tablespoon hot chilli paste
80ml white rice vinegar
2 tablespoons hoisin sauce
1 tablespoon soft brown sugar
2 teaspoons sesame oil
2 tablespoons soya bean oil
4 salmon steaks

Saucepan: combine the beer, ginger, garlic, spring onions, chives, coriander, chilli paste, rice vinegar, hoisin sauce, brown sugar and 1 teaspoon of the sesame oil. Bring to the boil. Keep stirring until the mixture reduces by half, and turns into a syrup.

Oven: preheat to 200°C.

Saucepan (large, deep): combine the soya bean oil with the rest of the sesame oil, and heat over medium heat. Place the salmon in the pan and sear on both sides. Remove from the heat and top the salmon with about a quarter of the glaze for each steak.

Baking dish: transfer the salmon to a baking dish.

Oven: bake the fish for about 5-7 minutes or until cooked to your liking. Garnish with the green parts of the spring onions, finely chopped, or chopped chives.

Saffron Fish Stew

Serves:	6
Preparation:	25-35 mins
Cooking:	25-35 mins

250ml beer (lager) – chef's tip: Steinlager Pure
1 tablespoon oil
1 medium onion finely chopped
3 cloves garlic crushed
1 celery stick thinly sliced
1 small fennel bulb thinly sliced
1 small leek thinly sliced
2 420gm tins tomatoes chopped with juice
4 cups fish stock
Pinch of saffron threads
200gm small new potatoes cubed
500gm raw prawns peeled and deveined
300gm firm white fish fillets
300gm salmon fillets
500gm mussels cleaned and debearded

Saucepan (large, deep): heat the oil over a low-medium heat. Add the onion, garlic, celery, fennel and leek and cook for about 10 minutes, stirring often, or until the vegetables soften.

Add the beer, chopped tomatoes, stock, saffron and potatoes. Bring to the boil. Immediately reduce heat and simmer, uncovered, for 10-12 minutes or until the potatoes are tender.

Add the prawns and fish, which should be cut into 2-3cm pieces. Simmer, uncovered, for 5 minutes.

Add the mussels and cover. Cook for 2-3 minutes or until the mussels open. Discard any shells that do not open. Serve.

'Beauty lies in the hands of the beerholder.'

- *Anonymous*

Fish Boil Up

Serves:	4
Preparation:	30-40 mins
Cooking:	20-30 mins

330ml beer (lager) – chef's tip: Speight's Summit
3 tablespoons oil
1 medium onion finely diced
100gm chorizo sausage cut into small cubes
400gm firm white fish fillets cut into 3cm pieces
200gm raw prawns peeled and deveined
800gm pipis or cockles
12 large mussels scrubbed and debearded
½ cup chicken stock
Juice of 8 limes
½ cup fresh coriander chopped
16 cherry tomatoes halved
1 red capsicum chopped
Salt and cracked black pepper to season

Saucepan (large, deep): heat the oil over a low-medium heat and saute the onion and chorizo sausage until they start to brown. Add the fish and prawns. Gently stir until the fish and prawns are browned on one side. Turn the fish, prawns and sausage and immediately add the shellfish. Cook for 1 minute and then add the beer.

Add the chicken stock and lime juice. Though it will be difficult to stir, do your best to mix the contents of the pan.

Cover and bring to the boil. Immediately reduce heat. Simmer, covered, until the shells have opened. Discard any shells that do not open.

Add the coriander, tomatoes, capsicum and salt and pepper to season. Simmer, uncovered, for 5 more minutes to reduce the broth.

Serving up

Serve in bowls with a sprig of coriander as garnish.

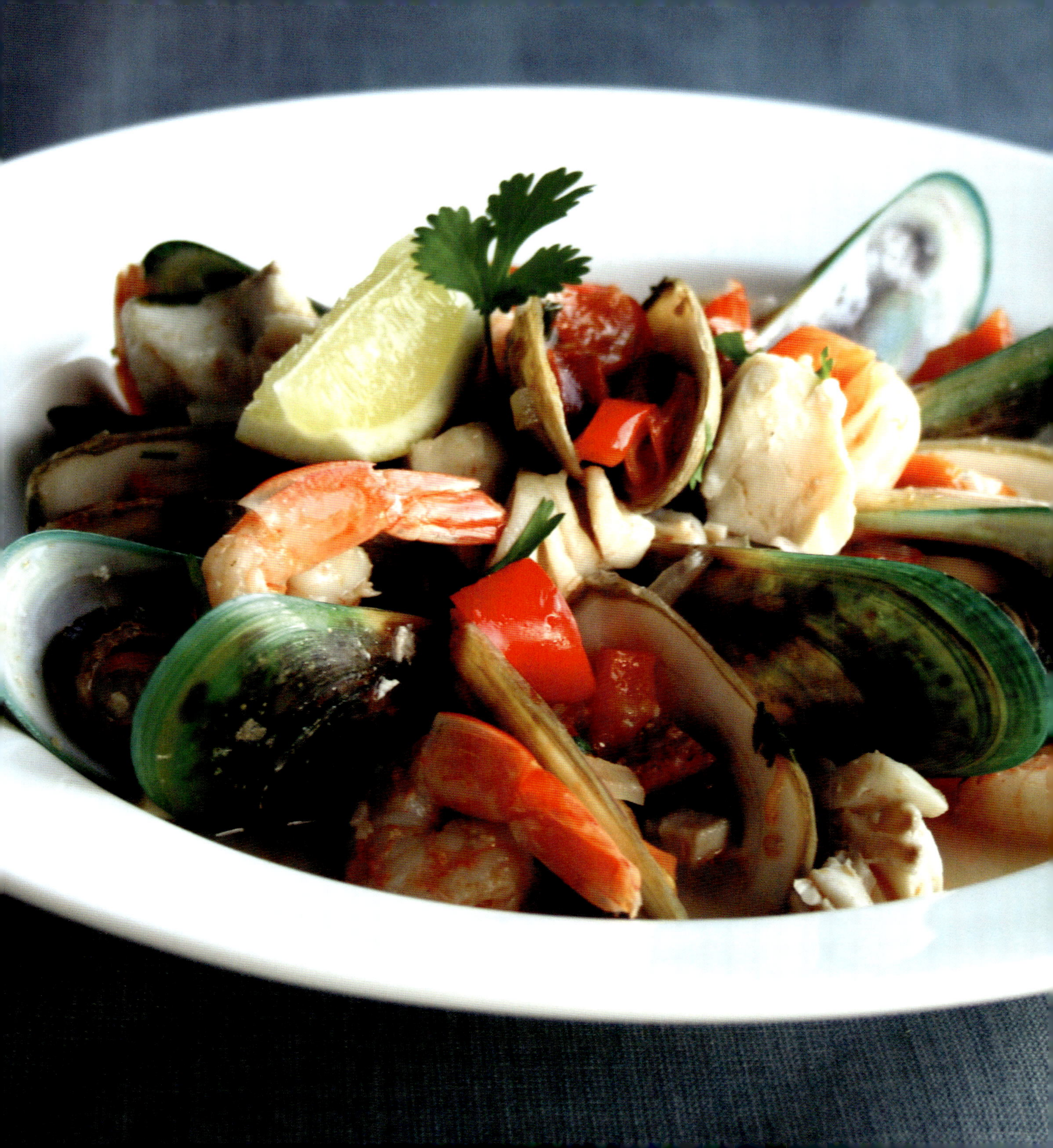

Smoked Salmon with Scrambled Eggs

Serves:	4
Preparation:	10-15 mins
Cooking:	7-10 mins

30ml beer (lager) – chef's tip: Export Gold
8 eggs
1 tablespoon cream
1½ tablespoons chives chopped
Salt and white pepper to season
2 teaspoons butter
8 strips smoked salmon
Cream cheese for spreading
Bread for toasting

This is a simple but tasty dish suited for weekend brunches or to start any day. While this recipe uses smoked salmon (which is freely available at supermarkets), you can substitute with other smoked fish.

Bowl: beat the eggs. Add the beer followed by the cream. Stir in half the chopped chives and add salt and pepper to season.

Fry pan: heat the butter over low-medium heat. When the butter starts to bubble slightly, pour in the eggs. Fold in the eggs but do not mix too vigorously.

Cook the eggs to your liking. They will continue to cook after removal from heat.

Serving up

Toast a suitable bread – sourdough (see recipe on page 29) works well with eggs – and smear with cream cheese. Spoon the eggs over the bread and top with 2 slices each of smoked salmon.

Garnish with the remaining chives and serve. Great with grilled tomatoes and hash browns.

Stews and casseroles

Oxtail Stew

Serves: 4
Preparation: 25-35 mins
Cooking: 2-3 hours

330ml beer (dark) – chef's tip: Monteith's Black
1.5kg oxtail
¼ cup all-purpose flour
2 tablespoons oil
2 teaspoons salt
1 teaspoon ground black pepper
1 medium onion diced
1 medium carrot peeled and sliced
2 sticks celery diced
1 baby leek diced
2 cloves garlic crushed
2 teaspoons of ginger crushed
2 tablespoons tomato paste
2½ tablespoons all-purpose flour
1½ cups beef stock
1 teaspoon of yeast extract – chef's tip: Marmite
1 bay leaf

Garnish with gremolata

2 teaspoons lemon zest
1 clove garlic finely chopped
4 tablespoons flat-leaf parsley finely chopped

It's important to seek out a decent piece of oxtail for this dish so scout around for a butcher who has trimmed off the fat first or be prepared to do so yourself.

Plate: dust with the flour and season with salt and pepper. Roll the portions of oxtail in the flour, shaking off any excess.

Stewing pot (large, deep): heat the oil over medium heat. Introduce the sections of oxtail to the pot, searing each side. If necessary, brown the oxtail pieces in stages, setting them aside on a plate to make way for the rest of the meat. When all the meat is seared, set aside.

Add the onions, carrots and celery to the stewing pot. Saute the vegetables for 3-4 minutes, until they have softened, and add the leek, garlic and ginger. Saute for another minute, and add the tomato paste. Stir continuously until all ingredients are well mixed.

Sieve the flour over the pot and stir to combine. Cook for 3 minutes while stirring all the time. Add the beer to the pot and increase the heat to medium-high. When the pot boils, cook for 5 minutes.

Add the beef stock, yeast extract and bay leaf and return the oxtail segments to the pot. Bring to the boil and immediately cover and reduce heat to a simmer. Keep on a low heat for at least 2 hours to get the most from the flavours in the stew. Skim off any excess oil every 30-40 minutes.

When the meat is tender, remove from the heat. Discard the bay leaf.

Bowl: to make the gremolata garnish, combine the lemon zest, garlic and flat-leaf parsley.

Serving up

Best served in bowls and garnished with gremolata. Goes well with mashed potato.

Oxtail Stew with gremolata garnish ▶

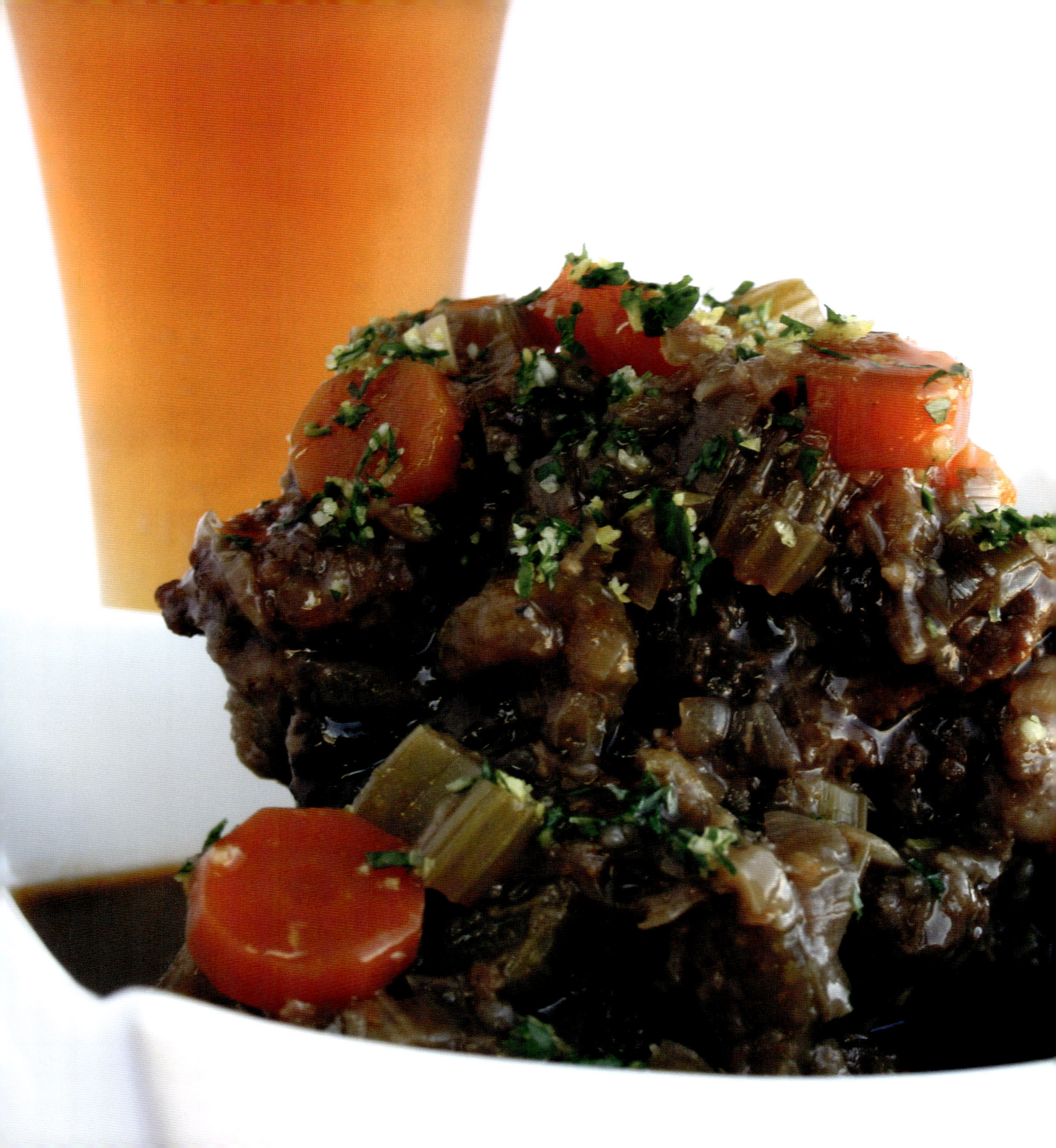

Sausage Casserole

Serves:	4
Preparation:	15-20 mins
Cooking:	1¼-1½ hours

330ml beer (lager or draught) – chef's tip: Tui
10-12 sausages, flavour of your choice
1 tablespoon oil
1 medium onion diced
2 cloves garlic crushed
350gm carrots roughly cut
500gm small new potatoes halved
1 420gm tin tomatoes chopped
1 teaspoon Worcestershire sauce
½ teaspoon dried thyme
½ teaspoon dried basil
2 beef stock cubes
Salt and cracked black pepper to season
Fresh parsley chopped (optional)

You can vary the flavours in this dish by choosing different types of sausage and experimenting with styles of beer.

Oven: preheat to 180°C.

Fry pan (large, deep): heat the oil over medium heat and add the sausages. Keep turning until they are browned. You do not need to fully cook the sausages as they will continue to cook when added to the casserole later. Set aside and allow to cool. Sweat the onions in the fry pan over low-medium heat until soft and translucent. Add the garlic and cook for 1-2 minutes. Add the carrots and potatoes and cook for 2 minutes.

Add the beer, tomatoes, Worcestershire sauce, thyme and basil. Crumble in the beef stock cubes.

Bring to the boil and immediately transfer to a casserole dish.

Board: when the sausages have cooled sufficiently, cut them into 3cm pieces.

Casserole dish: add the sausages to the casserole dish and mix with the other ingredients. Top up the liquid in the dish with boiling water to just cover the ingredients. Season with salt and pepper. Cover.

Bake for 1-1¼ hours or until the vegetables are tender, stirring occasionally.

Serving up

Serve in a bowl and garnish with parsley (optional).

Duck Stew

Serves:	4-6
Preparation:	20-25 mins
Cooking:	55-70 mins

330ml beer (lager or draught) – chef's tip: Tui
2kg duck pieces
1 cup all-purpose flour
1 teaspoon salt
1 tablespoon dried marjoram
60gm butter
3 cups hot chicken stock
1 clove garlic crushed
½ medium onion
1 bay leaf
2 strips of lemon peel
2 sticks celery cut into quarters
3 sprigs fresh parsley
½ teaspoon fresh thyme chopped
2 tablespoons cornflour
3 tablespoons beer (any)
Salt and cracked black pepper to season

Bowl 1 (medium): sift 1 cup of flour with the salt and marjoram into the bowl and mix. Roll the pieces of duck in the flour and lightly coat. Shake off excess flour and set aside.

Fry pan (large, deep): heat the butter in the pan over a medium-high heat. When it is bubbling, add the duck and brown it on all sides. Add the beer and allow it to boil for 1 minute.

Add the hot chicken stock, followed by the garlic, onion, bay leaf, lemon peel, celery, parsley and thyme. Stir well. Bring to the boil. Immediately reduce to a low heat and simmer, covered, for 40-45 minutes or until the duck is tender.

Remove the bay leaf, celery, onion and lemon peel. Using a slotted spoon, skim the fat off the surface of the stew.

Bowl 2 (small): mix the cornflour and 3 tablespoons of beer to form a smooth paste. Add gradually to the stew, allowing the gravy to thicken to the consistency you prefer. Season with salt and pepper.

Serving up

A tasty way of serving this dish is to line a bowl with fresh baby spinach and pour the stew over it. This wilts the spinach. Add some steamed carrots over the top of the stew.

Venison Chilli

Serves:	4
Preparation:	20-30 mins
Cooking:	1¾-2 hours

250ml beer (dark) – chef's tip: Black Mac
2 tablespoons oil
900gm venison cut into 2cm cubes
1 large onion diced
½ cup red capsicum chopped
½ cup green capsicum chopped
3 tablespoons ground cumin
1 tablespoon paprika
1 teaspoon cayenne pepper
1 tablespoon celery salt
1 tablespoon dried oregano
3 cloves garlic crushed
½ fresh red chilli finely chopped and deseeded (optional)
1 bay leaf
1½ cups tomato puree
1½ cups beef stock
3 cups cooked red kidney beans
Salt and cracked black pepper to season

Garnish

2 tablespoons fresh coriander chopped
2 thin slices of red capsicum
Sour cream

Saucepan (large, deep): heat the oil over a medium-high heat. When hot, add enough of the venison cubes to cover the bottom of the pan and sear the meat on all sides to trap in flavour.

Bowl: transfer the seared meat to a bowl and replace with more venison until all the meat is seared. Set aside all the meat in the bowl.

Lower the heat to low-medium and sweat the onion in the saucepan for 1-2 minutes. Add the capsicums and saute until the onion is soft and translucent. Return the venison to the pan. Add the cumin, paprika, cayenne pepper, celery salt, oregano and garlic and stir together, cooking for 2 minutes. Add the fresh red chilli (optional).

Add the bay leaf, tomato puree, beer, beef stock and kidney beans and increase the heat until the contents reach boiling. Reduce to a low heat, cover and leave to simmer for 1 hour. Then uncover and increase heat to low-medium, simmering for 30 minutes to reduce most of the liquid.

Season with salt and cracked black pepper.

Serving up

Garnish with the chopped coriander. Serve with wild rice.

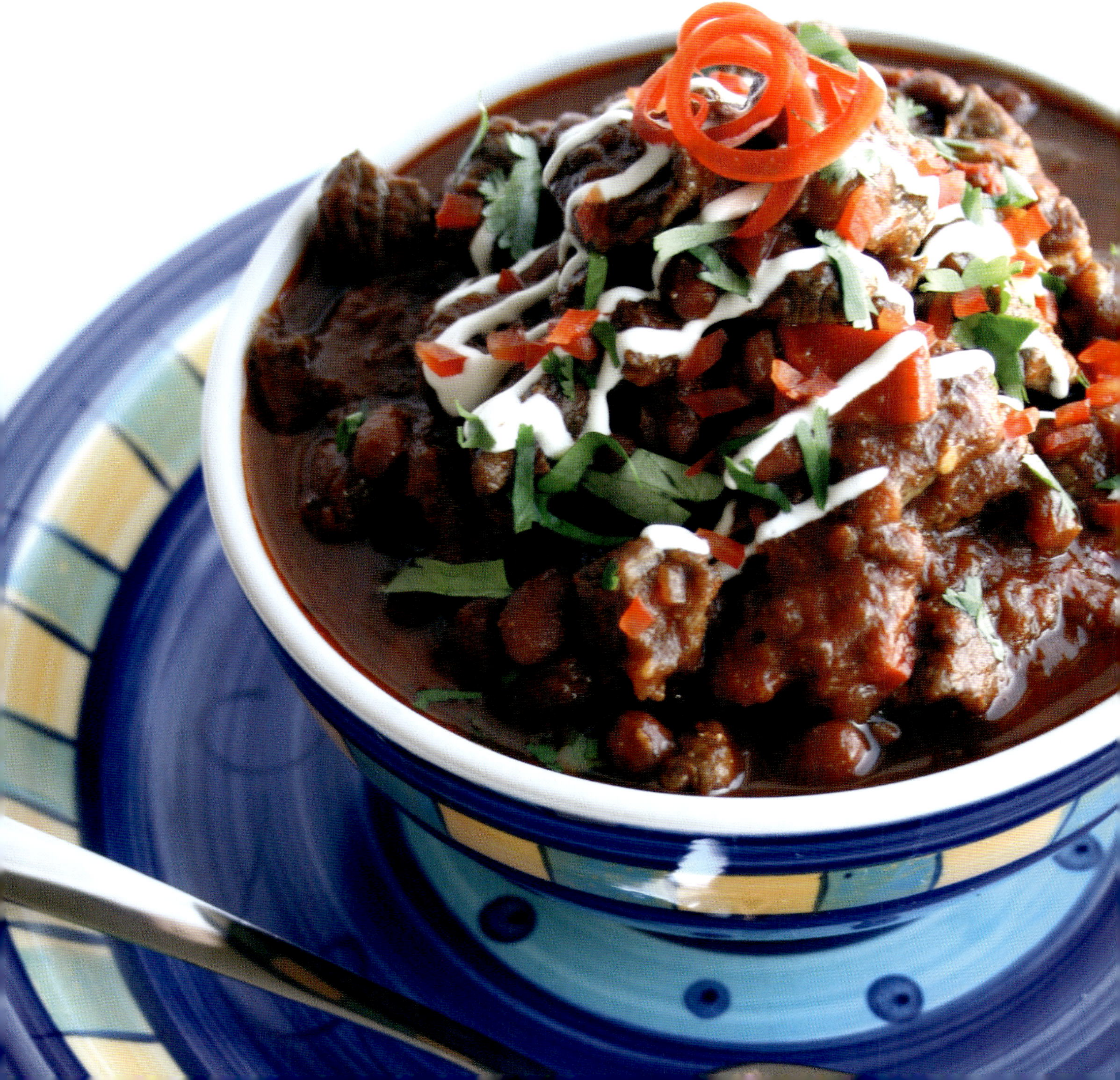

Beef Stroganoff

Serves:	4
Preparation:	15-20 mins
Cooking:	1-1¼ hours

410ml flat beer (any) – chef's tip: DB Draught
2 tablespoons butter
1 tablespoon oil
1 cup spring onions sliced
2 cloves garlic crushed
225gm mushrooms sliced
900gm lean beef steak cut into thin strips
1½ teaspoons salt
2 teaspoons tomato sauce
1 teaspoon Worcestershire sauce
¼ teaspoon paprika
3 tablespoons all-purpose flour
¾ cup sour cream
Salt and cracked black pepper to season

Perfect comfort food, especially during winter, this dish can be served alone or with your favourite choice of carbs.

Saucepan (large, deep): heat the butter and oil over low-medium heat. Saute the spring onions, garlic, mushrooms and beef strips until the meat and mushrooms brown.

Add the salt, tomato sauce, Worcestershire sauce, paprika and 355ml of the beer. Bring to the boil. Immediately reduce heat and simmer, covered, for 45 minutes.

Bowl: gradually add the remaining beer to the flour and mix to make a smooth paste. You may not need to use all the beer to achieve this.

Saucepan: gradually add flour-beer mixture to the saucepan, stirring constantly, to thicken the gravy. Add the sour cream and warm through. Be careful not to allow the stroganoff to boil as this will separate the cream. Season with salt and pepper and serve.

'When I read about the evils of drinking, I gave up reading.'

- *Henry Youngman*

Kiwi Casserole

Serves:	4
Preparation:	20-30 mins
Cooking:	1-1¼ hours

240ml beer (lager) – chef's tip: Speight's Summit
125gm bacon
450gm pork and fennel sausages (or Italian)
2 cloves garlic crushed
3¼ cups chicken stock low salt
2 420gm tins cannellini beans drained and rinsed
2 cups of cooked boneless chicken shredded
3 teaspoons fresh rosemary chopped
½ cup Parmesan cheese grated
Salt and cracked black pepper to season
2 cups seasoned fresh bread crumbs

For seasoned bread crumbs, just add salt and pepper to the fresh bread crumbs.

Oven: preheat to 200°C.

Fry pan (large, deep): brown the bacon over medium heat until it starts to crisp. Transfer to a paper towel to drain the bacon fat. When cool enough, roughly cut the bacon into pieces.

Add the sausages to the pan and brown, adding a little oil if necessary. Remove from the pan and cut the sausages into 2-3cm chunks. Return the sausage pieces to the pan and add the garlic. Stir and gradually increase heat until the garlic is sizzling but not turning brown.

Add the beer and continue to stir while the fluid almost completely reduces. This should take a couple of minutes at full heat.
Add the stock and bring back to the boil. Add the beans, chicken and rosemary and reduce heat to simmer. Allow about 5 minutes for the ingredients to heat through.

Casserole dish (oven proof): transfer the contents to a casserole dish. Add the bacon, stir in the Parmesan cheese and season with salt and pepper. Sprinkle a layer of bread crumbs evenly across the surface.

Oven: bake the casserole for about 25 minutes, until the crumbs are brown and crisp. Remove from the oven and allow to stand for 5 minutes.

Serving up

Best served in bowls. Grind some more black pepper if it's to your taste.

Sausage & Capsicum Stew

Serves:	4
Preparation:	15-20 mins
Cooking:	40-50 mins

220ml beer (lager or draught) – chef's tip: Tui
1½ tablespoons oil
800gm spicy sausages
1 large onion sliced
2 cloves garlic chopped
1 red capsicum chopped
1 green capsicum chopped
80gm tomato paste
1 420gm tin tomatoes chopped and drained
¾ cup beef stock
1 teaspoon dried oregano
1 teaspoon dried coriander
½ teaspoon hot pepper sauce (optional) – chef's tip: Kaitaia Fire
Salt and cracked black pepper to season

Garnish (optional)

Chopped parsley or chopped chives

This simple stew bursts with flavour and suits those who like their food hot and spicy.

Saucepan (large, deep): heat the oil over medium heat. Add the sausages and keep turning until they are fully browned. They do not need to be fully cooked at this stage as they will continue to cook later. Remove the browned sausages from the pan and set aside on a plate.

Add the onions, garlic, red and green capsicums. Stir and cook for 2 minutes. Add the beer and bring to the boil. Stir in the tomato paste, drained tomatoes and beef stock. Add the oregano, coriander, hot pepper sauce (optional) and salt and pepper to taste.

Bring back to the boil. Immediately reduce heat and simmer for 5 minutes.

Board: cut the sausages into thirds and add to the pan. Stir, cover and simmer for 20-25 minutes or until the sausages are cooked and the onions and capsicums are tender. Remove the cover and simmer for 5 minutes or until the stew has thickened.

Serving up

This goes well with mash and your favourite vegetables. Garnish with chopped parsley or chives.

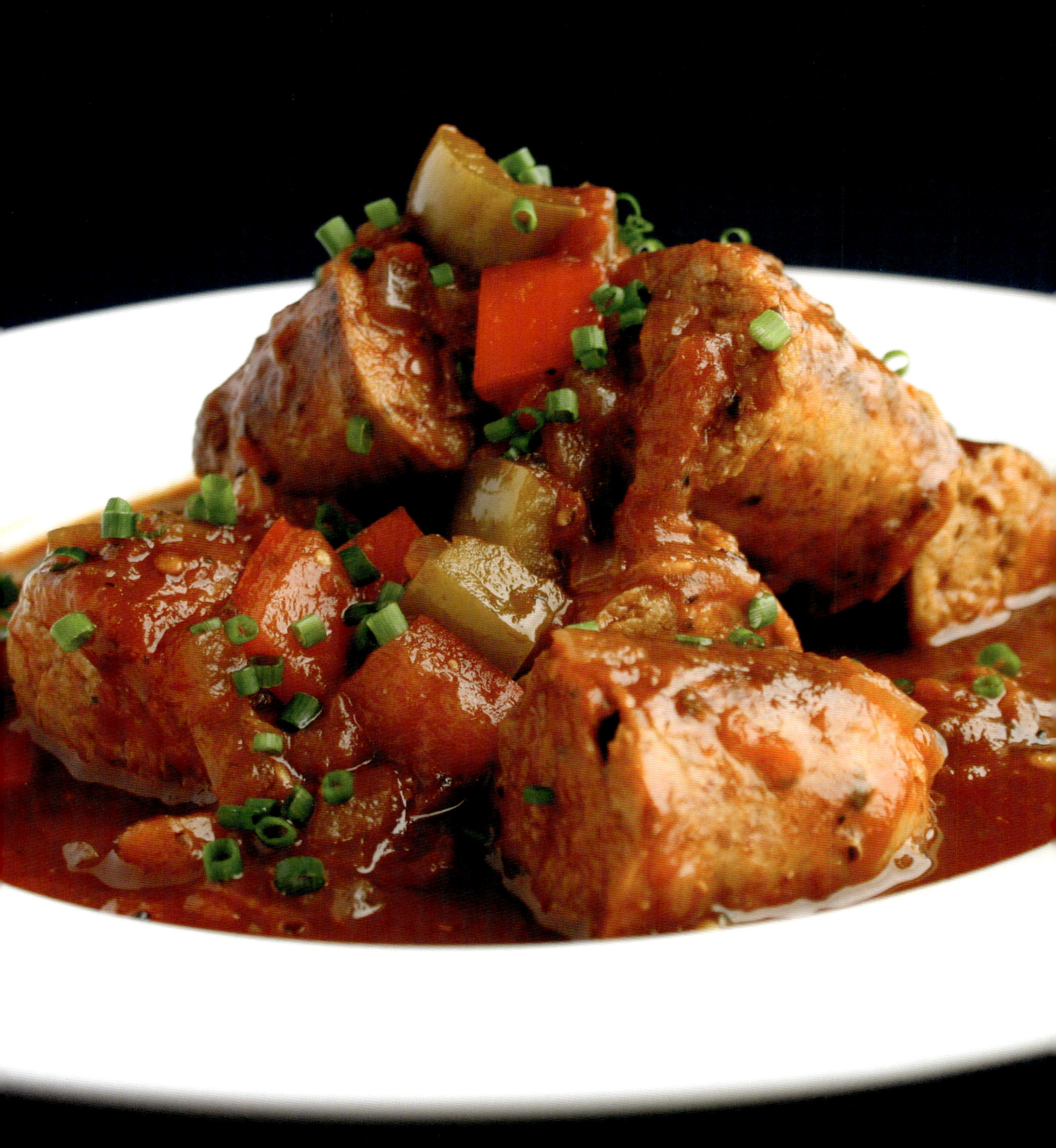

Beef & Kumara Casserole

Serves:	4-6
Preparation:	35-40 mins
Cooking:	2-2¼ hours

250ml beer (dark) – chef's tip: Monteith's Black
1kg beef steak cut into 2cm pieces
½ cup all-purpose flour
2 tablespoons oil
1 large onion diced
2 bacon rashers chopped
2 cloves garlic crushed
2 tablespoons tomato paste
1 bay leaf
1 tablespoon fresh thyme chopped
2 cups beef stock
1 420gm tin tomatoes chopped
¼ cup Worcestershire sauce
500gm kumara roughly chopped
300gm carrots roughly chopped
1 large red capsicum roughly chopped
Salt and cracked black pepper to season
Fresh parsley chopped (for garnish)

This stove top casserole is the ideal solution for those who want a change from 'meat and potato' basics.

Bowl: coat the beef in flour. Shake off excess.

Fry pan (large, non-stick): heat 1 tablespoon of oil over medium-high heat and cook the beef in batches until browned. Set aside.

Pot (large, deep): heat 1 tablespoon of oil over low-medium heat. Sweat the onion for 2-3 minutes. Add the bacon and cook for 2-3 minutes, and then add the garlic for 2 minutes. Stir occasionally.

Add the tomato paste and stir for 1 minute. Add the beef to the pot. Add the bay leaf and thyme.

Pour in the beer, beef stock, tomatoes and Worcestershire sauce. Mix well and bring to the boil. Reduce heat and simmer, covered, for 1 hour. Stir occasionally.

Add the kumara, carrots and capsicum and mix well. Simmer, uncovered, for 30 minutes or until the beef and vegetables are tender, stirring occasionally. Season with salt and pepper.

Serving up

Garnish with a sprinkling of chopped fresh parsley when serving up in bowls.

Beef & Vegetable Stew

Serves:	4
Preparation:	20-25 mins
Cooking:	1¾-2 hours

330ml beer (dark) – chef's tip: Black Mac
2 tablespoons oil
1kg beef steak cut into 2cm pieces
½ cup all-purpose flour
2 cloves garlic crushed
2½ cups beef stock
2 bay leaves
1 teaspoon dried thyme
3 medium carrots cut into 1cm slices
250gm mushrooms halved
6 pickling onions halved
8 small new potatoes halved
Salt and cracked black pepper to season

Bowl: coat the beef in flour. Shake off excess.

Fry pan (large, non-stick): heat the oil over medium-high heat and cook the beef in batches until browned. Transfer the beef to a stew pot.

Stew pot (large, deep): combine the beef with the rest of the ingredients. Stir well. Cover. Bring to the boil. Immediately reduce heat to low and simmer covered, stirring occasionally, for about 1½ hours or until the beef is tender. Remove the bay leaves and discard.

Season with salt and pepper and serve.

Pork Boil Up

Serves:	4
Preparation:	10-15 mins
Cooking:	1¾-2¼ hours

330ml beer (lager) – chef's tip: Export Gold
1kg pork bones
2 tablespoons salt
6 medium potatoes peeled and roughly chopped
3 medium kumara peeled and roughly chopped
Salt and cracked black pepper to season
1 bunch watercress

Stew pot (large, deep): place the pork bones in the pot. Add the beer and salt. Bring the fluid level to the top of the bones with cold water. Bring to the boil, cover and leave to simmer for 1½ hours.

While simmering, occasionally check to make sure the bones are always covered by liquid, adding small amounts of water if necessary.

After the bones have cooked for 1½ hours, add the potatoes and kumara to the pot. Season with salt and pepper. Keep on the boil until the vegetables are tender.

Tear the watercress in half, and then half again, and add to the pot for the last 5 minutes of cooking.

Chicken Chilli Stew

Serves:	4
Preparation:	20-30 mins
Cooking:	35-40 mins

60ml beer (lager) – chef's tip: Mac's Gold
2 tablespoons oil
1kg chicken breasts cut into 2-3cm pieces
1 medium onion diced
3 cloves garlic crushed
½ red capsicum chopped
½ teaspoon ground cumin
1 teaspoon dried oregano
¼ teaspoon chilli powder
½ fresh red chilli finely chopped
¾ cup chicken stock
1 420gm tin tomatoes chopped
1 400gm tin red kidney beans, rinsed and drained

Saucepan (large, deep): heat half the oil over medium heat. Add the chicken pieces in batches and brown. Set aside.

Add remaining oil. Over low-medium heat, sweat the onion for 3-4 minutes until it is soft. Add the garlic and capsicum and cook for 2 minutes. Add the cumin, oregano, chilli powder and fresh chilli and keep stirring.

Return the chicken to the pan. Add the beer, stock and tomatoes. Bring to the boil. Immediately reduce heat and simmer, covered, for about 25 minutes or until the sauce starts to slightly thicken.

Add the kidney beans and simmer uncovered for 5 minutes while the beans warm through.

Pork Stew

Serves:	6-8
Preparation:	15-20 mins
Cooking:	55-65 mins

330ml beer (lager) – chef's tip: Mac's Gold
1½ tablespoons oil
1½ teaspoons salt
900gm pork fillet, trimmed of fat and cut into 2-3cm cubes
1 medium onion chopped
2 cloves garlic crushed
1 red chilli finely chopped and deseeded
2 teaspoons ground cumin
1 teaspoon dried oregano
1 420gm tin tomatoes chopped
1 red capsicum chopped
4 tablespoons fresh coriander finely chopped
Salt and cracked black pepper to season

Stew pot (large, heavy base): heat 1 tablespoon of oil over a medium heat until hot. Lightly salt the pork and add to the pot. Cover and cook for 15-20 minutes, stirring often, until the pork has browned. Remove the pork and reserve for later.

Add the rest of the oil and sweat the onion for 2-3 minutes until it is soft and translucent. Add the garlic and saute for 2 minutes. Add the chilli, cumin and oregano and stir for 2-3 minutes to unlock their flavours.

Add the beer and heat until the liquid reduces by about half. Add the tomatoes and capsicum.

Bring the stew to the boil. Reduce to a low heat and simmer, uncovered, for 25-30 minutes or until the pork is tender and the sauce has thickened. Stir in the coriander.

Season with salt and pepper. Garnish with more fresh coriander.

Meats and mains

Lamb Shanks

Serves:	4
Preparation:	20-30 mins
Cooking:	2¼ hours

330ml beer (draught) – chef's tip: Speight's Gold Medal Ale
4 lamb shanks trimmed
½ cup all-purpose flour
Salt and cracked black pepper to season
3 tablespoons oil
3 large onions sliced
1 420gm tin tomatoes chopped
1 teaspoon dried thyme
1 teaspoon dried basil

The key to this dish is not over-stressing on the quantities listed in the ingredients – trust your own judgement to get the right consistency of gravy. There's no such thing as a standard-sized lamb shank (or knuckle) so either choose four big enough to feed a foursome or add more if needed.

You may need more than one can/bottle of beer – just make sure there's sufficient fluid in the pot to just cover the shanks. Remember, you can always add more fluid – it's difficult to take out once added.

Plastic bag: to prepare the shanks, dab them dry, if necessary, with paper towels and place them in a plastic bag containing the sieved flour, with salt and pepper. Give the bag a gentle shake and remove the shanks, leaving behind the excess flour.

Fry pan: heat the oil over low-medium heat and sweat the onions until soft.

Dish: remove the onions to a dish and reserve for later.

Fry pan: add the shanks until the meat turns brown and flavour is sealed in. Transfer the shanks and onions to a deep pot.

Stew pot (large, deep): add the tomatoes, thyme, basil and beer, ensuring the fluid just reaches the top of the shanks. Season with salt and pepper and cover. As soon as boiling point is reached, reduce to simmer for 2 hours or until the meat is tender and almost ready to fall off the bone. Occasionally turn the shanks and stir.

Serving up

Delicious with mashed potato, round beans and carrots. Use the left over liquid from the stew pot as the gravy for this dish.

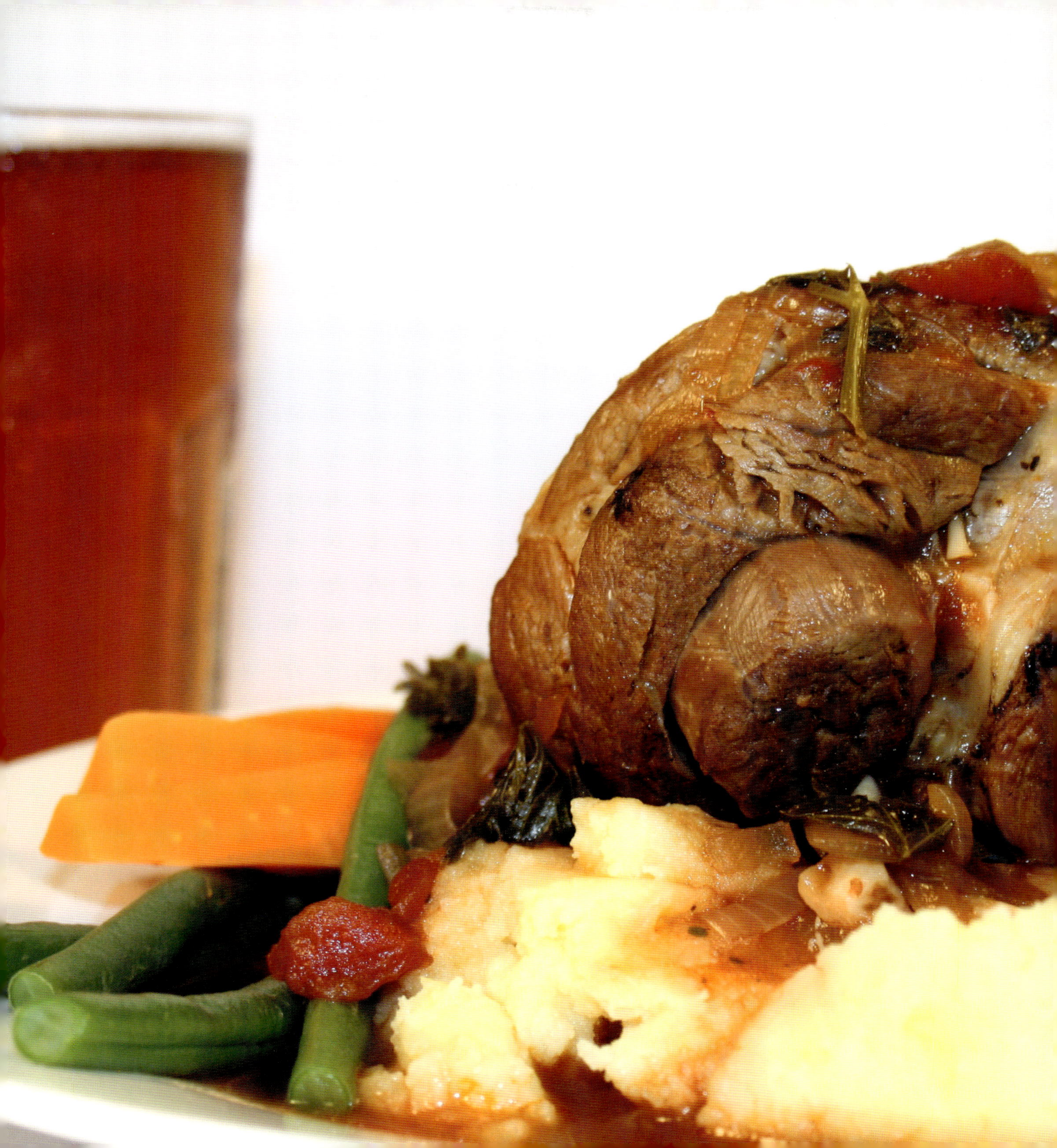

Chicken Paella

Serves:	4
Preparation:	10-15 mins
Cooking:	30-35 mins

375ml beer (lager or draught) – chef's tip: Tui
2 tablespoons oil
2 chicken breasts, skinless cut into 2-3cm pieces
Salt and cracked black pepper to season
100gm chorizo sausage diced
1 medium onion finely diced
3 cloves garlic crushed
1 teaspoon ground cumin
1 teaspoon turmeric
½ teaspoon chilli powder
1½ cups long grain rice
1 420gm tin Italian seasoned tomatoes chopped
1 cup frozen peas
¼ cup dry sherry

Saucepan (large, deep): heat the oil over medium heat. Season the pieces of chicken with salt and pepper. Add them to the pan and brown on all sides. Add the chorizo sausage, stir and cook for 2 minutes. Add the onion and cook for 2 minutes. Stir in the garlic, cumin, turmeric and chilli powder and cook for 1 minute.

Add the rice and mix well with the other ingredients. Cook for 1 minute. Add the tin of tomatoes and beer. Increase the heat until the liquid just starts to bubble. Reduce the heat, cover and simmer for 20 minutes.

Add the frozen peas, mixing them into the paella. Cover and stand for 5 minutes. Fluff up the paella with a fork and sprinkle the sherry over the dish. Serve.

'I work till beer o'clock.'

- *Stephen King*

Steak Pie

Serves:	4
Preparation:	20-25 mins
Cooking:	2-2½ hours

250ml beer (dark) – chef's tip: Monteith's Black
1.1kg-1.2kg stewing beef cut into 2cm cubes
½ cup all-purpose flour
1 teaspoon salt
½ teaspoon ground black pepper
2 tablespoons oil
1 large onion diced
2 cloves garlic crushed
3 tablespoons water
1½ tablespoons tomato paste
1 cup beef stock
1 tablespoon Worcestershire sauce
1 teaspoon ground black pepper
2 teaspoons fresh thyme chopped
Grated cheese (optional)

Pastry

Sheets of frozen pastry
1 egg lightly beaten

Bowl 1 (large): toss the cubes of beef in the flour, salt and pepper until well coated. Shake off any excess.

Oven: preheat to 180°C.

Saucepan (large, deep): heat the oil over medium-high heat. Add the pieces of beef in batches and sear them for about 3 minutes or until they are browned on all sides. Transfer the seared meat to a plate.

Add the onion and garlic to the pan and saute over low-medium heat for 4-5 minutes or until the onion and garlic are soft and translucent. Stir in the 3 tablespoons of water. Add the tomato paste and stir well for 1 minute. Return the beef and juices to the pan. Add the beef stock, Worcestershire sauce, pepper and thyme. Add the beer and mix well. Bring to the boil. Remove from the heat.

Casserole dish (ovenproof): transfer the contents of the saucepan to the dish. Bake in the oven, covered, for 1½-1¾ hours, stirring occasionally, or until you have thick gravy and tender meat. Remove and stand to cool.

Pie dishes (4, ovenproof): fill each with the meat and gravy filling. If you wish, add a sprinkling of grated cheese on top of the filling. Cover each dish with a layer of pastry (following the pastry manufacturer's instructions on how to thaw and use).

Oven: preheat to 200°C.

Bowl 2 (small): beat the egg and lightly brush the pastry.

Oven: bake the pies long enough to heat the filling and for the pastry to puff up and turn golden brown (refer pastry manufacturer's instructions). This usually takes about 20 minutes.

Serving up

Serve with mashed potatoes and your choice of vegetables.

Corned Silverside

Serves:	8
Preparation:	10-15 mins
Cooking:	3¼-3¾ hours

330ml beer (lager or draught) – chef's tip: Speight's Gold Medal Ale
1 small onion roughly chopped
2 carrots peeled and cut into 2cm pieces
2 sticks celery chopped
1 bay leaf
½ teaspoon whole cloves
4 black peppercorns
1.5kg corned silverside
1 teaspoon honey

Stew pot (large, deep): place the onion, carrot, celery, bay leaf, cloves and peppercorns in the pot. Add the silverside and the beer and add sufficient water to cover the meat. Add the honey and mix well. Cover and bring to the boil. Reduce the heat and simmer, covered, for 2½-3 hours or until the meat is tender.

Check every half hour and turn the meat in the liquid. Skim any surface fat from the liquid. When cooked, carefully remove the meat from the pot and discard the other contents.

Serving up

Try mashed potato on the side and maybe a dash of mustard or mustard sauce which contrasts well with the sweetness of the meat. For suitable vegetables to accompany this meat, try the recipes for carrots or cabbage (see recipe on page 54).

Curried Tomato Chicken

Serves:	4
Preparation:	10-15 mins
Cooking:	1¼-1½ hours

160ml beer (lager or draught) – chef's tip: Tui
4 chicken breasts, boneless, skinless, halved
2 tablespoons oil
1 onion chopped
1 clove garlic chopped
1 300gm tin condensed tomato soup
1½ teaspoons curry powder
1 teaspoon dried basil
½ teaspoon ground black pepper
¼ cup Parmesan cheese grated

Oven: preheat to 180°C. Place the chicken breasts in a greased baking dish.

Fry pan (large, deep): heat the oil over low-medium heat. Sweat the onion for 3-4 minutes. Add the garlic and cook for 2-3 minutes until the onion is soft and translucent. Stir in the beer, soup, curry powder, basil and pepper. Bring the mix to the boil and immediately reduce heat to low.

Simmer for about 10 minutes then pour over the chicken breasts.

Oven: bake the chicken for 50-60 minutes. Turn the chicken and sprinkle with Parmesan cheese for the last 10 minutes of baking.

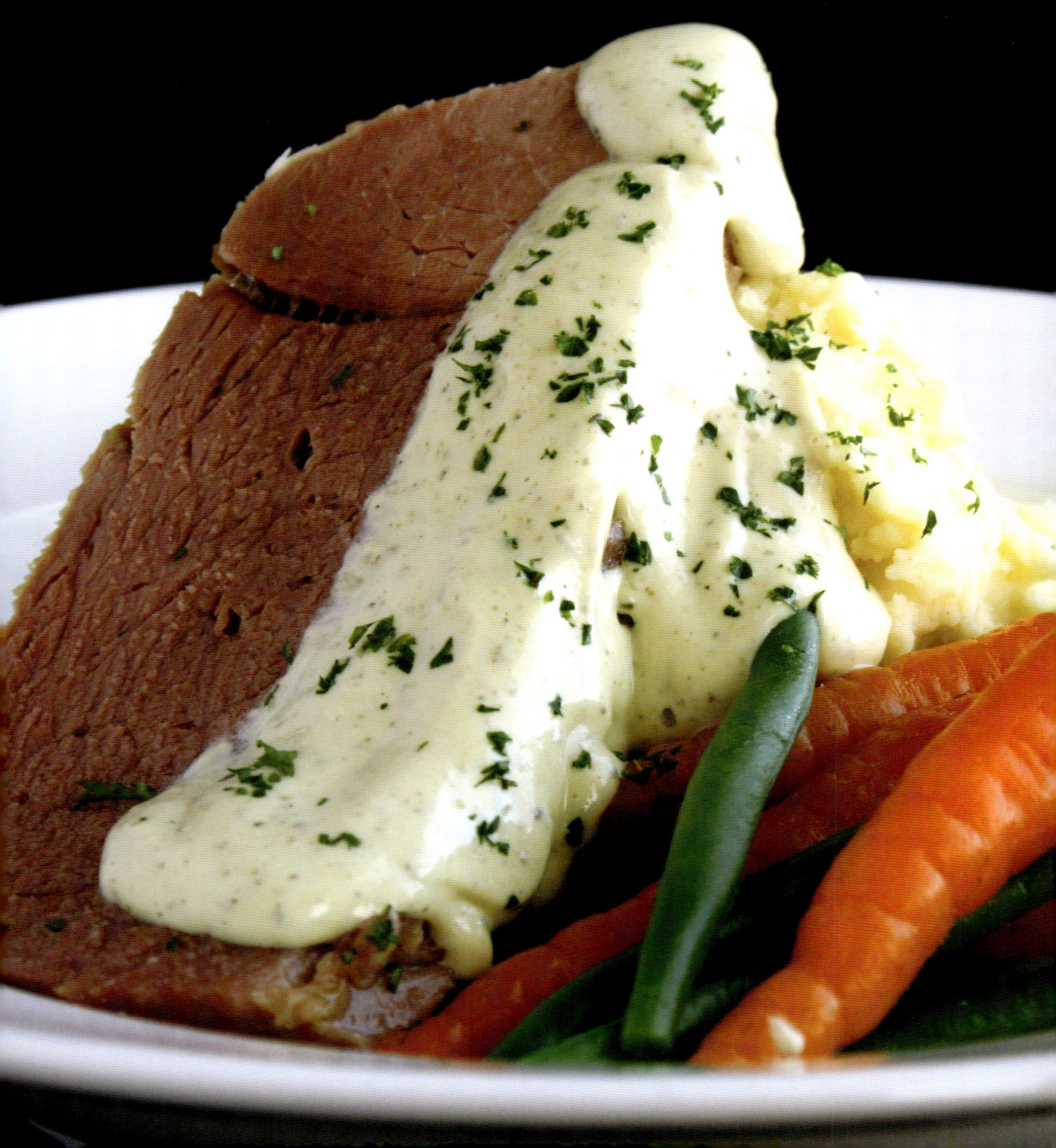

Crumbed Venison Steaks

Serves:	4-6
Preparation:	15-20 mins
Refrigeration:	2 hours
Cooking:	8-12 mins

30ml beer (dark) – chef's tip: Black Mac
6 eggs lightly beaten
1 clove garlic sliced
Salt and cracked black pepper to season
1-2 cups seasoned bread crumbs
1kg venison steak
2 tablespoons butter
4 tablespoons oil

Bowl 1: combine the eggs and beer. Add the garlic, salt and cracked black pepper. Mix well.

Baking dish (shallow): place the venison in a single layer in the dish and cover with the marinade from Bowl 1. Cover and refrigerate for 2 hours, turning the meat in the dish after 1 hour.

Bowl 2: add the bread crumbs. Remove the venison from the baking dish and roll each steak in the bread crumbs, ensuring they become fully covered.

Fry pan (large): heat the butter and oil over medium-high heat. When the pan is hot, fry the steaks until they are cooked the way you like them.

Roast Herb Chicken

Serves:	4
Preparation:	15-20 mins
Cooking:	1¼-2 hours

330ml beer (lager or draught) – chef's tip: Tui
2 tablespoons fresh basil chopped
2 tablespoons fresh thyme chopped
2 tablespoons fresh marjoram chopped
½ teaspoon cracked black pepper
1 teaspoon salt
1 teaspoon paprika
3 cloves garlic crushed
1 cup fresh herbs of your choice chopped
1 chicken
2 tablespoons oil

The key to this dish is basting the chicken with the herb and beer mix every 15-20 minutes during cooking.

Bowl: combine the basil, thyme, marjoram, pepper, salt, paprika and garlic. Mix well and then rub it over the chicken, rubbing some of the mix inside its cavity. Place the fresh herbs (of your choice) inside the chicken.

Brush the oil over the chicken.

Oven: preheat to 180°C.

Roasting dish: place the chicken in the dish and pour the beer over it. Roast the chicken for 20 minutes for every 450gm it weighs, plus an extra 10-20 minutes.

Baste the chicken with the beer in the roasting dish every 15-20 minutes or add more beer if necessary.

Jambalaya

Serves:	6
Preparation:	20-30 mins
Cooking:	40-55 mins

330ml beer (lager or draught) – chef's tip: Tui
4 chorizo sausages
1 tablespoon oil
3 chicken breasts skinless and boned cut into 2cm cubes
2 medium onions diced
4 cloves garlic crushed
2 sticks celery chopped
1 green capsicum chopped
1 red capsicum chopped
2 cups long-grain rice
1½ cups chicken stock
1½ teaspoons dried thyme
1½ teaspoons dried oregano
½ teaspoon cayenne pepper
¼ teaspoon red chilli flakes
½ teaspoon salt
½ teaspoon cracked black pepper
1 420gm tin tomatoes chopped
350gm raw prawns peeled and deveined

Pot: prick the chorizo sausages with a fork and place them in the pot. Submerge them in the beer and bring to the boil. Reduce to a low heat and simmer for 8-10 minutes.

Remove the sausages from the pot and allow to cool. When cool, cut them into slices. Let the beer cool in the pot and reserve.

Saucepan (large): heat the oil over medium-high heat and add the chicken pieces. Saute them for about 3 minutes or until they are lightly browned on all sides. Add the slices of chorizo sausage and cook for 3-4 minutes, stirring every minute or so. Remove the chicken and sausage from the pan and set aside.

Reduce the heat to low-medium. Add the onion to the pan and sweat for 3-4 minutes until soft. Add the garlic and cook for 1-2 minutes. Add the celery, green capsicum and red capsicum and stir well. Cook for 2-3 minutes.

Add the rice and stir for 1 minute. When the rice is evenly distributed, add the chicken stock and 1 cup of the reserved beer. Add the thyme, oregano, cayenne pepper, chilli flakes, salt and pepper. Mix well.

Return the chicken and sausage to the pan and add the tin of chopped tomatoes. Stir and simmer, uncovered, for 20-25 minutes while most of the liquid is absorbed. Stir every 5 minutes or so.

Finally, add the prawns and stir them into the other ingredients, allowing them to cook for about 5 minutes. Serve when all the prawns are pink and have warmed through.

Shepherd's Pie

Serves:	4
Preparation:	20-30 mins
Cooking:	1-1¼ hours

250ml beer (dark) – chef's tip: Black Mac
2 tablespoons oil
1 medium onion diced
3 cloves garlic crushed
1kg minced beef
1 tablespoon tomato paste
1 420gm tin tomatoes chopped
1 teaspoon dried oregano
1 teaspoon dried basil
2 tablespoons Worcestershire sauce
2 beef stock cubes
1 large carrot chopped into 1cm pieces
1 cup frozen peas thawed
Salt and cracked black pepper to season
900gm potatoes peeled and quartered
¼ cup milk
2 tablespoons butter
Parmesan cheese (optional)

Garnish

Chopped parsley

Saucepan (large): heat the oil over medium heat. Sweat the onion and garlic until the onion is soft and translucent. Add the minced beef to the pan and keep turning it for about 8-10 minutes until it is browned throughout. Stir in the tomato paste and cook for 1-2 minutes.

Add the beer, chopped tomatoes, oregano, basil and Worcestershire sauce. Stir well. Crumble in the beef stock cubes. Bring to the boil. Immediately reduce heat.

Add the carrots and simmer for 30-40 minutes or until the fluid has reduced to a smooth gravy. Add the thawed peas and stir in. Season with salt and cracked black pepper.

Pot (large): while the meat is simmering, boil your potatoes. Keep them warm so you can mash them with the milk and butter when your meat and gravy are ready.

Oven: preheat to 200°C.

Casserole dish (ovenproof): place the mince mixture in the dish. Carefully spoon the mashed potato over the top of the meat, using a fork to spread it evenly.

Bake the potato-topped pie for 10-15 minutes and then place under the grill to brown.

Serving up

If you like a crust on the top of the pie, add a sprinkle of grated Parmesan cheese before grilling. This gives the dish a golden finish. Garnish with chopped parsley.

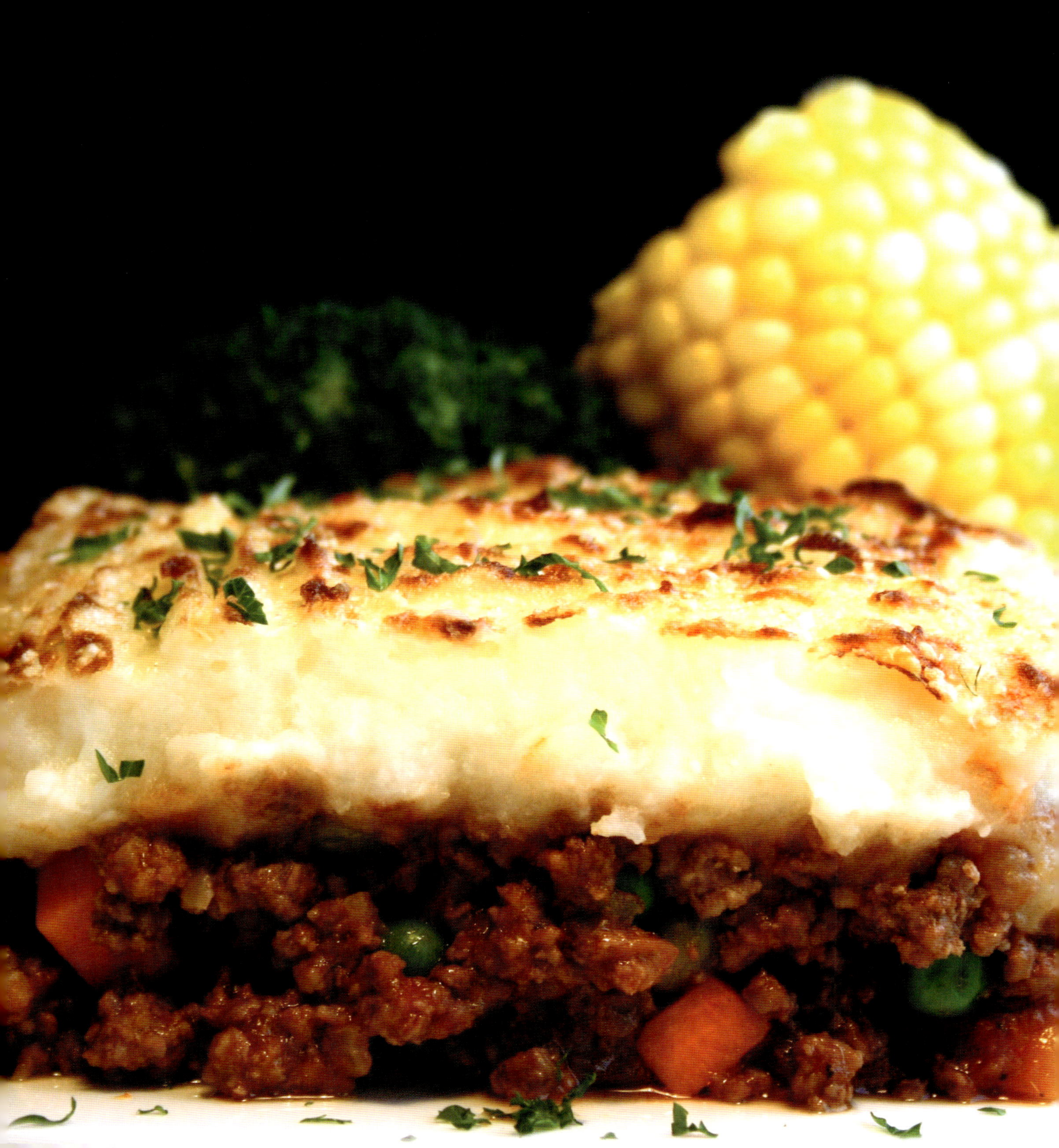

Beef, Mushroom & Bacon Pie

Serves:	4
Preparation:	20-30 mins
Cooking:	2-2½ hours

250ml beer (dark) – chef's tip: Monteith's Black
1kg stewing beef cut into 2cm cubes
½ cup all-purpose flour
1 teaspoon salt
½ teaspoon ground black pepper
2 tablespoons oil
1 medium onion diced
150gm bacon diced
2 cloves garlic crushed
125gm button mushrooms sliced
1½ tablespoons tomato paste
3 tablespoons water
1 cup beef stock
1 tablespoon Worcestershire sauce
1 tablespoon fresh thyme leaves

Pastry

Sheets of frozen pastry
1 egg lightly beaten

Bowl 1 (large): toss the cubes of beef in the flour, salt and pepper until well coated. Shake off any excess.

Oven: preheat to 180°C.

Saucepan (large, deep): over medium-high heat, heat the oil. Add the pieces of beef in batches and sear them for about 3 minutes or until they are browned on all sides. Transfer the seared meat to a plate.

Add the onion to the pan and saute for about 3 minutes over low-medium heat. Add the bacon and cook for 3 minutes. Add the garlic and cook for 2 minutes, before adding the mushrooms. Stir well and cook for 1-2 minutes. Add the 3 tablespoons of water and the tomato paste. Stir well for 1 minute. Return the beef and juices to the pan. Add the beef stock, Worcestershire sauce and leaves from the thyme. Add the beer and mix well. Bring to the boil. Remove from the heat.

Casserole dish: transfer the contents of the saucepan to the dish. Bake in the oven for 1½-1¾ hours, stirring occasionally, or until you have thick gravy and tender meat. Remove and stand to cool.

Pie dishes (4, ovenproof): fill each with the meat and gravy filling. Cover each dish with a layer of pastry (following the pastry manufacturer's instructions on how to thaw and use).

Oven: preheat to 200°C.

Bowl 2 (small): beat the egg and lightly brush the pastry.

Oven: bake the pies long enough to heat the filling and for the pastry to puff up and turn golden brown (refer pastry manufacturer's instructions). This usually takes about 20 minutes.

Serving up

Surely there has to be a bottle of tomato sauce on the table – whether it's needed or not!

Lamb Rogan Josh

Serves:	4-6
Preparation:	20-25 mins
Cooking:	1½-1¾ hours

330ml beer (lager) – chef's tip: Export Gold
1 large onion chopped
2 teaspoons fresh ginger peeled and chopped
6 cloves garlic chopped
1 teaspoon ground cinnamon
2 teaspoons ground cumin
2 teaspoons ground coriander
1 tablespoon paprika
1 teaspoon chilli powder
1 teaspoon salt
1 tablespoon tomato paste
2 tablespoons oil
1kg trimmed lamb cut into 2-3cm pieces
¼ teaspoon cardamom seeds

Food processor: blend the onion, ginger, garlic, the ground spices, salt and tomato paste until smooth.

Saucepan (large): heat the oil over medium heat. Add the lamb and cardamom seeds. Sear the lamb, ensuring it's browned on all sides. Cook in batches if necessary.

Stir in the spicy mixture from the food processor. Cook for 5 minutes, stirring often.

Add the beer. Bring to the boil. Immediately reduce heat and simmer, covered, for 1-1¼ hours, stirring occasionally. Take off the heat when the sauce has thickened and the lamb is tender.

Stand for 5 minutes before serving.

Dry Beef Curry

Serves:	6
Preparation:	10-15 mins
Cooking:	1¾-2 hours

60ml beer (lager or draught) – chef's tip: Tui
2 tablespoons oil
2 medium onions diced
4 cloves garlic crushed
2 teaspoons ginger peeled and grated
2 teaspoons ground cumin
2 teaspoons ground coriander
2 teaspoons ground garam masala
1 teaspoon ground turmeric
1.5kg beef steak cut into 2-3cm pieces
¾ cup beef stock
¼ cup fresh coriander chopped
6 tablespoons plain natural yoghurt

Saucepan (large, deep): heat the oil over low-medium heat. Sweat the onions for 2-3 minutes until they soften. Add the garlic, ginger and ground spices, while stirring.

Add the beef. Stir to thoroughly coat the pieces of beef with the onion and spices.

Add the beer and stock. Bring to the boil. Immediately reduce heat and simmer, covered, for about 1 hour. Stir occasionally.

Continue to simmer, uncovered, for 30 minutes, stirring occasionally, until the liquid reduces and the beef is tender. This will result in a dry curry.

Serving up

Garnish with chopped coriander and add a spoonful of plain natural yoghurt to each dish.

Beer Can Chicken

Serves:	4+
Preparation:	5-10 mins
Cooking:	depends on size of chicken

330ml can of beer (any lager or draught)
1 large chicken
1 tablespoon salt
1 tablespoon ground black pepper

This is a fun way to cook a chook and an opportunity to experiment with different flavours.

The cooking method requires you to cook the chicken upright (with its legs and parson's nose at the bottom) either in a kettle-style barbecue or in a large oven. It would pay to check the size of your oven/barbecue and your bird before you try this.

You are also going to cook the bird while it 'sits' on a beer can. This can be achieved in two ways. The easy option is to buy a piece of equipment from your local barbecue store that's designed for this (they are not expensive). Otherwise, you'll need to use great care and use a couple of spuds, or similar, to help prop the chicken into position in the roasting tray.

Once you've sorted out your technique, cooking the bird is a delight.

First, empty half the can of beer. Then stab a few holes in the upper half of the can with a screwdriver or similar, making sure no parts of the can come loose in the process.

Insert the can into the chicken's rear end. Rub the outer of the chicken with salt and pepper. Cook the chicken for the appropriate time period, depending on size. This may take slightly longer than normal using this method so check the chicken is fully cooked.

Carefully remove the can, without spilling the beer, and throw it away – do not try to drink it (it will be bitter). Rest the chicken for 10 minutes before serving.

That's the basic Beer Can Chicken recipe. But you can vary the formula as much as you want. Use your favourite marinade or herb/spice rub to flavour the bird and add a dash to the beer can. Try different beers for different outcomes. Or mix a splash of sauce into the can – like Worcestershire sauce – and the beer will help it steam its flavour into the meat. Whatever your choice of flavour, you'll have created a talking point for your next barbecue!

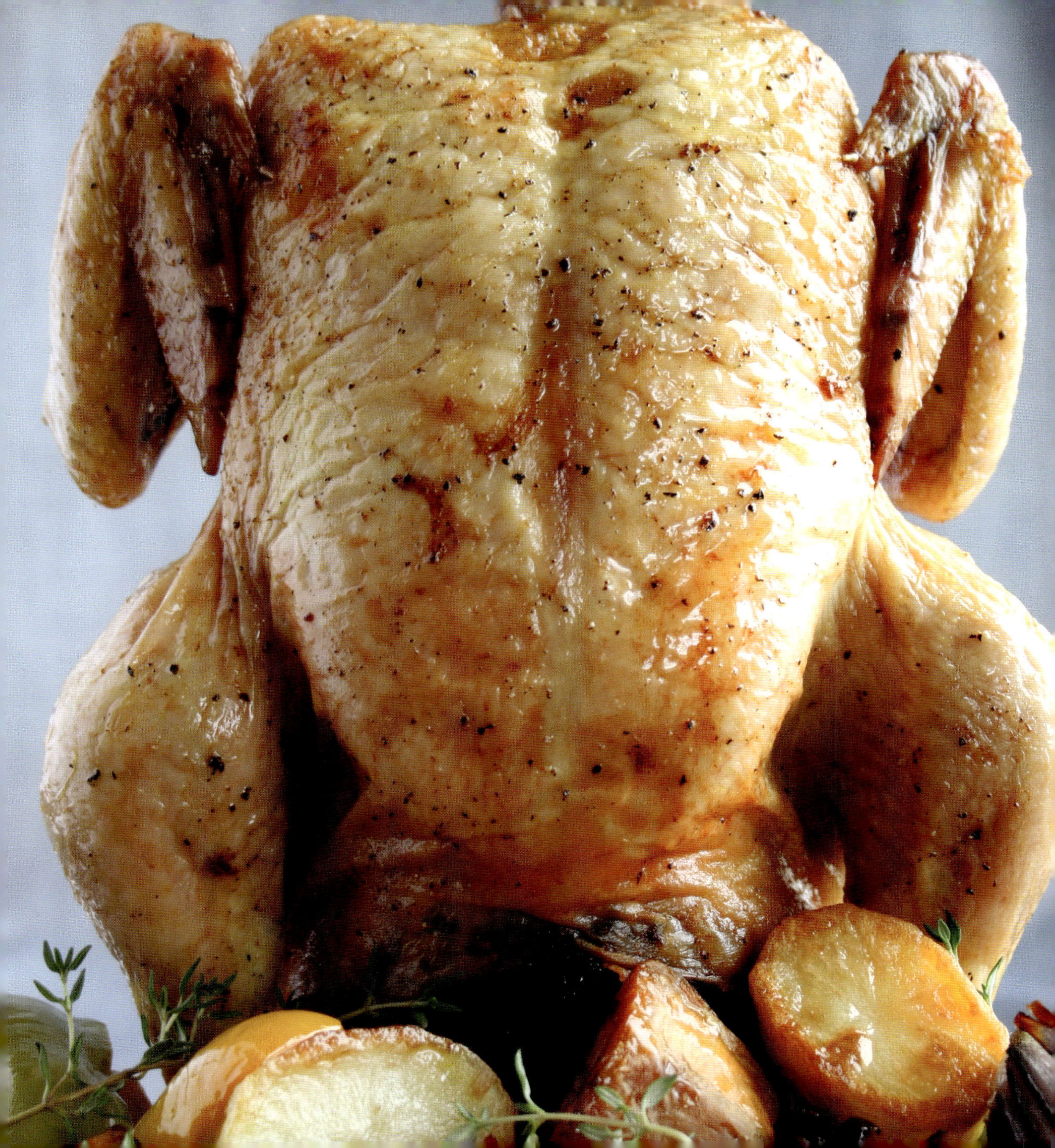

Burger & Onions

Serves:	4
Preparation:	10-15 mins
Cooking:	25-40 mins

Burger

60ml beer (draught) – chef's tip: Lion Red
675gm ground beef mince
2 cloves garlic crushed
¼ cup red capsicum finely diced
2 tablespoons Dijon mustard
Salt and cracked black pepper
1 cup cheese grated

Onions

180ml beer (draught) – chef's tip: Lion Red
1 tablespoon butter
1 teaspoon oil
1 large onion thinly sliced
1 tablespoon sugar

Burger Patties

Bowl: combine the beer, beef mince, garlic, capsicum, mustard and season with salt and pepper. Mix well. Make the mixture into 4 burger patties. Set aside.

Onions

Saucepan: heat the butter and oil over a low-medium heat. Add the onions and cook for 5-6 minutes, stirring frequently, until they are soft. Add the beer and sugar. Increase the heat to medium. Cook for about 15 minutes while the beer is absorbed by the onions and they become lightly browned. Stir regularly.

Cover the onions with foil and keep them hot while you cook the patties.

BBQ or fry pan: cook the burger patties for about 4-6 minutes each side or until you are happy they are cooked to your taste.

When the patties are cooked, flip them so their hot side is facing upwards. Sprinkle ¼ cup of grated cheese on top of each one and the heat from the patty will start to melt the cheese. The cheese might not fully melt until you place the hot onions on top of each patty when assembling the burgers.

Serving up

Place the patties on toasted buns and smother with the hot onions and your choice of other fillings. The burgers go well with Tangy Tomato Sauce (see recipe on page 65).

Beef Stir-fry

Serves:	4
Preparation:	10-15 mins
Cooking:	10-15 mins

350ml beer (lager or draught) – chef's tip: Tui
40ml hoisin sauce
2 tablespoons brown sugar
1 teaspoon sesame oil
¼ cup beef stock
700gm beef steak cut into thin strips
1 tablespoon oil
2 cups broccoli florets halved
1 medium green capsicum sliced
1 medium red capsicum sliced
1 medium orange capsicum sliced
70gm snow peas topped and tailed
2 spring onions sliced

This is a quick and easy meal and like many Asian-inspired dishes is best served with rice or noodles.

Bowl (large): combine the beer, hoisin sauce, brown sugar, sesame oil and beef stock. Mix well to dissolve the sugar. Add the meat to the bowl and toss through the sauce. Remove the beef and set aside. Reserve the sauce.

Saucepan (large, non-stick), or wok: heat the oil over medium-high heat. Add the beef and stir-fry for 2-3 minutes to sear. Remove and set aside on a plate. Add the sauce and bring to the boil for 1 minute. Add the broccoli for 2 minutes, stirring continuously. Add the capsicums and snow peas. Stir for 1½-2 minutes to ensure the vegetables are evenly cooked.

Return the seared beef to the pan/wok. Add the spring onions. Stir long enough to warm through and serve.

Serving up

Pour the stir-fry over your choice of noodles or rice.

'Mmmm, beer.'
- Homer Simpson

Sausages & Garlic Mash

Serves:	4
Preparation:	25-30 mins
Cooking:	40-45 mins

Sausages

660ml beer (lager or draught) – chef's tip: Lion Red
12 sausages, your choice of flavour (try to find sausages that are not split at their ends as they will hold their shape better)

Mash

330ml beer (lager) – chef's tip: Mac's Gold
900gm potatoes peeled and quartered
2 cloves garlic halved
45gm butter
½ cup milk
¾ cup mild Cheddar cheese grated
1 tablespoon fresh chives chopped
1 tablespoon fresh parsley chopped
Salt and pepper to season

Sausages

Pot (large): place the sausages in the pot. Cover with beer and top up with cold water, if necessary, to cover the sausages. Bring to the boil. Reduce heat to low and simmer, uncovered, for 15-18 minutes to ensure the sausages are cooked.

Remove the sausages and allow them to cool on paper towels.

BBQ or fry pan: cook the pre-cooked sausages for 5-7 minutes, allowing them to brown and heat through.

Mash

Pot (large): put the potatoes in the pot with the beer and garlic. Cover them with water and bring to the boil. Reduce heat and simmer for 20-25 minutes or until tender. Drain the potatoes.

Pot (small): add the butter and milk and warm until the butter is melted.

Pot (large): while the potatoes are still hot, add the butter and milk and start mashing the potatoes and garlic. Once the butter and milk have been absorbed, add the cheese and continue to mash until smooth.

Add the chives and parsley and whip the mash with a fork for 1-2 minutes to achieve a really smooth finish. Season with salt and pepper.

Serving up

Sit three of the sausages atop a mound of mash and add lashings of onion gravy (see recipe on page 70).

Macaroni Cheese with Bacon

Serves:	4
Preparation:	20-30 mins
Cooking:	50-75 mins

470ml beer (lager) – chef's tip: Export Gold
400gm uncooked elbow macaroni
90gm butter
2 teaspoons oil
1 large onion diced
1 clove garlic crushed
4 tablespoons all-purpose flour
1 teaspoon salt
½ teaspoon pepper
1 cup milk
1 cup cream
450gm Cheddar cheese grated
150gm bacon cooked and diced

Saucepan 1: cook the macaroni to the directions on its packet. Be careful not to overcook. Drain well. Cool.

Oven: preheat to 180°C.

Saucepan 2: heat the butter and oil over low-medium heat and sweat the onion until it is soft and translucent. Add the garlic and cook for 2-3 minutes. Stir in the flour, salt and pepper. Add the beer and stir constantly for 2-3 minutes until the mix thickens. Gradually add the milk and cream, stirring constantly. When the mixture has thickened, remove from the heat. Stir in 325gm of the grated cheese. Add the drained macaroni and bacon.

Baking dish: pour the macaroni cheese into a greased dish and top with the remaining cheese.

Oven: bake for 30 minutes, uncovered, or until the cheese bubbles and browns.

Spag Bol

Serves:	4-6
Preparation:	20-30 mins
Cooking:	1¼-1½ hours

125ml beer (dark) – chef's tip: Black Mac
2 tablespoons oil
1 large onion chopped
3 cloves garlic crushed
1kg beef mince
Salt and cracked black pepper to season
50gm tomato paste
½ cup beef stock
2 420gm tins tomatoes chopped
2 teaspoons sugar
1 teaspoon dried oregano
Pinch nutmeg
Parmesan cheese grated
Fresh basil (garnish)

Saucepan (large): heat the oil over low-medium heat and sweat the onion until soft. Add the garlic, cook for 1 minute and add the minced beef, stirring the meat well to break apart any lumps. Increase the heat to medium-high. Season with salt and pepper. Once the liquid has evaporated and the meat has browned, stir in the tomato paste.

Mix well. Add the beer and cook for 1 minute. Add the beef stock. Mix well. Add the remaining ingredients, except for the basil and Parmesan cheese. Bring to the boil. Reduce heat and simmer for 50-60 minutes, stirring occasionally. Season with salt and pepper.

Serving up

Serve with your favourite pasta, grated Parmesan cheese and garnish with fresh chopped basil.

Garlic Roast Beef

Serves:	5-6
Preparation:	15-20 mins
Refrigeration:	2 hour minimum
Stand time:	15-20 mins
Cooking:	1½-2 hours

180ml beer (draught) – chef's tip: Speight's Gold Medal Ale
2 tablespoons oil
3-4 cloves garlic crushed
½ teaspoon salt
¼ teaspoon ground black pepper
1.4kg-1.6kg topside beef roast
1 crumbled beef stock cube
2 tablespoons all-purpose flour

This recipe turns a regular roast beef into something special with beer playing a key role at the start and finish of making the dish.

Bowl 1: combine the beer, oil, garlic, salt and pepper, mixing well.

Bowl 2 (large): stand the beef in a bowl and pierce the meat in a number of fleshy places with a fork. Pour the mixture from Bowl 1 over the beef, spooning it into the flesh where it has been pierced. Cover and refrigerate for 2 hours, occasionally turning the meat. Remove from the refrigerator to stand at room temperature for about 15-20 minutes before it goes in the oven.

Oven: preheat to 170°C.

Roasting dish (large): place the meat on a rack in the dish, with its fatty side up, and sprinkle with the crumbled beef cube. Gently rub the crumbs into the meat, especially over the fatty parts.

Reserve the marinade.

Oven: roast the meat for 1½ to 2 hours or until it is cooked to your liking. Remove from the oven, cover with foil and stand for 15-20 minutes before carving. While it is standing, it's time to make the gravy.

Roasting dish: drain the oil from the dish and discard. Using a wooden spatula, scrape the meat drippings from the dish and add them to the reserved marinade. Top up the marinade with water so you have 1 cup of liquid.

Place the roasting dish on the stove top over a low heat, stirring in the flour. Gradually add marinade to the dish, stirring continuously and scraping any meat residue into the gravy. The mixture should turn into a tasty brown gravy, reflecting the flavour of the meat, beer and garlic in the marinade. Keep stirring until the gravy is thick.

If you prefer thinner gravy, add a small amount of water to the dish and stir until you get the consistency you like.

Sweet as

Tipsy Fruitcake

Serves:	14-16
Preparation:	25-35 mins
Stand time:	1 hour
Cooking:	2½-2¾ hours

330ml beer (dark) – chef's tip: Black Mac
1kg your choice of mixed dried fruit chopped
225gm unsalted butter softened
1 cup brown sugar firmly packed
3 large eggs at room temperature
3 tablespoons brandy plus more for brushing the cake
Juice and zest from 1 medium orange
Zest from 1 lemon
¾ cup ground almonds
1 cup chopped walnuts and chopped pecans
2 cups all-purpose flour
1 teaspoon baking powder
¼ teaspoon salt

Pot: boil the beer in the pot. Remove from heat and add the chopped dried fruit (chef's tip: dried apricots, apples, raisins, pitted dates). Stand for 1 hour, stirring occasionally. Drain.

Bowl 1: using an electric mixer, beat the butter and sugar until light and fluffy. Add the eggs one at a time, beating well. Add the brandy, juice and zest of the orange and zest of the lemon. Fold in the almonds, walnuts and pecans. Fold in the fruit from the pan after draining any excess liquid.

Bowl 2: combine the sifted flour, baking powder and salt. Fold this into Bowl 1. Mix well.

Springform pan (round, 20cm): line the base and sides with greased paper ensuring the paper rises 5cms above the rim of the pan. Fill with cake mix and smooth the surface with a spatula.

Oven: preheat to 160°C. Bake for 1 hour. Reduce the temperature to 150°C and bake for 1½ hours or until a skewer inserted into the middle of the cake emerges clean. Remove from the oven and pan. Stand to cool. Prick small holes in the cake and brush with brandy every few days, and pack in plastic wrap and foil to store.

Cocoa Cake

Serves:	10-12
Preparation:	5-10 mins
Cooking:	50-55 mins

330ml beer (dark) – chef's tip: Black Mac
3 cups all-purpose flour
2 teaspoons baking soda
2 cups caster sugar
½ cup cocoa
1 teaspoon salt
¾ cup oil
4 teaspoons vinegar
1 teaspoon vanilla extract
½ cup cold water

Oven: preheat to 180°C.

Bowl: sift the flour, baking soda, sugar, cocoa and salt into a bowl.

Make a well in the mixture and add the oil, vinegar and vanilla extract. Lightly mix. Pour in the beer and add the water. Continue mixing and stir well.

Cake tin (square, 22cm): pour into the greased tin.

Oven: bake for 50-55 minutes or until a skewer inserted into the cake comes out clean.

Chocolate Chip & Walnut Cake

Serves:	6-8
Preparation:	10-15 mins
Cooking:	1-1¼ hours

180ml beer (lager) – chef's tip: Mac's Gold
1½ cups caster sugar
170gm unsalted butter
3 eggs
1½ teaspoons vanilla extract
2 cups sour cream
3 cups all-purpose flour
½ teaspoon baking powder
1½ teaspoons baking soda
Pinch salt
¾ cup chocolate chips
¾ cup walnuts chopped
½ cup caster sugar
2 tablespoons ground cinnamon

Oven: preheat your oven to 175°C.

Bowl 1: combine the 1½ cups of sugar and butter in a bowl. Cream until light and fluffy. Add the eggs, one at a time. Blend well. Add the vanilla extract and sour cream. Blend until creamy. Add the sifted flour, baking powder, baking soda, salt and beer. Blend well.

Bowl 2: in a separate bowl, combine the chocolate chips, walnuts, remaining sugar and cinnamon. Add this mixture to Bowl 1. Mix well. Pour the cake batter into a greased large ring tin.

Ring tin (large): bake for 1-1¼ hours or until a skewer inserted into the cake emerges clean.

Remove the cake tin from the oven and allow to cool fully before turning out the cake onto a plate. Top with your favourite icing.

Apple Crumble

Serves:	4-6
Preparation:	15-20 mins
Cooking:	50-65 mins

250ml beer (lager) – chef's tip: Export Gold
2 cups all-purpose flour
1 cup brown sugar firmly packed
170gm unsalted butter melted
½ cup quick cooking oats
1 cup caster sugar
3 tablespoons cornflour
1 teaspoon vanilla extract
6 medium apples peeled, cored and thinly sliced

Oven: preheat to 180°C.

Bowl: sift the flour into the bowl and add the brown sugar, melted butter and oats. Mix well with a wooden spoon until crumbs form.

Baking dish (square, 22cm): grease the dish and layer half the crumbs in the bottom.

Saucepan: mix the caster sugar, cornflour and beer. Heat over low-medium heat and cook until thickened, stirring constantly. Add the vanilla. Add the apple slices to the saucepan, gently stirring to coat them in the beer/vanilla mix. Spread this mixture over the crumbed base and sprinkle remaining crumbs over the top.

Oven: bake for 50-55 minutes until the top is brown. Serve hot.

Chocolate Mousse

Serves:	6-8
Preparation:	30-35 mins
Cooking:	10-15 mins
Refrigeration:	4 hours minimum

185ml beer (dark) – chef's tip: Monteith's Black
1 cup cream
230gm semi-sweet or bitter-sweet chocolate chopped
50gm unsalted butter
¼ cup caster sugar
3 large eggs separated
Pinch of cream of tartar

This recipe requires a fair amount of whipping and beating so use an electric beater or be prepared for a bit of a workout.

Bowl 1: whip the cream until soft peaks form. Refrigerate.

Double boiler: using a double boiler, or a small pot with 3cm of water, bring to the boil and immediately reduce heat so the water simmers. Place a metal or glass bowl over the pot, making sure it does not touch the water. Combine the chocolate, butter and sugar in the bowl. Use the indirect heat to melt the chocolate with the butter and sugar, using a high-heat spatula to work the mixture until it is smooth. Stir in the beer and whisk in the egg yolks. Remove from the heat for 2 minutes before adding the chilled cream.

Bowl 2: beat the egg whites with a pinch of cream of tartar until stiff peaks form. Fold the whites into the chocolate and cream mixture.

Dishes: spoon the mousse into small serving dishes and chill before serving. Don't be tempted to use large serving dishes as this may spoil the setting of the mousse.

Chocolate Truffles

Makes:	about 15
Preparation:	10-15 mins
Refrigeration:	1-2 hours
Cooking:	8-10 mins

90ml beer (dark) – chef's tip: Speight's Old Dark
90gm unsalted butter
225gm plain dark chocolate
125gm icing sugar
125gm ground almonds
30gm raisins chopped
Unsweetened cocoa powder for dusting

Double boiler: using a double boiler, or a small pot with 3cm of water, bring to the boil and immediately reduce heat so the water simmers. Place a metal or glass bowl over the pot, making sure it does not touch the water. Add the butter and chocolate and gently melt them. Do not overheat the chocolate as it will become sticky and impossible to work with.

When the chocolate and butter are melted, stir in the beer. Stir in the icing sugar, ground almonds and raisins. Mix well. Allow to cool and then refrigerate until the mixture sets.

Roll the mixture into balls slightly smaller than a golf ball. Chill. Then gently roll them in cocoa powder and place in paper cases. Chill again and serve from the refrigerator.

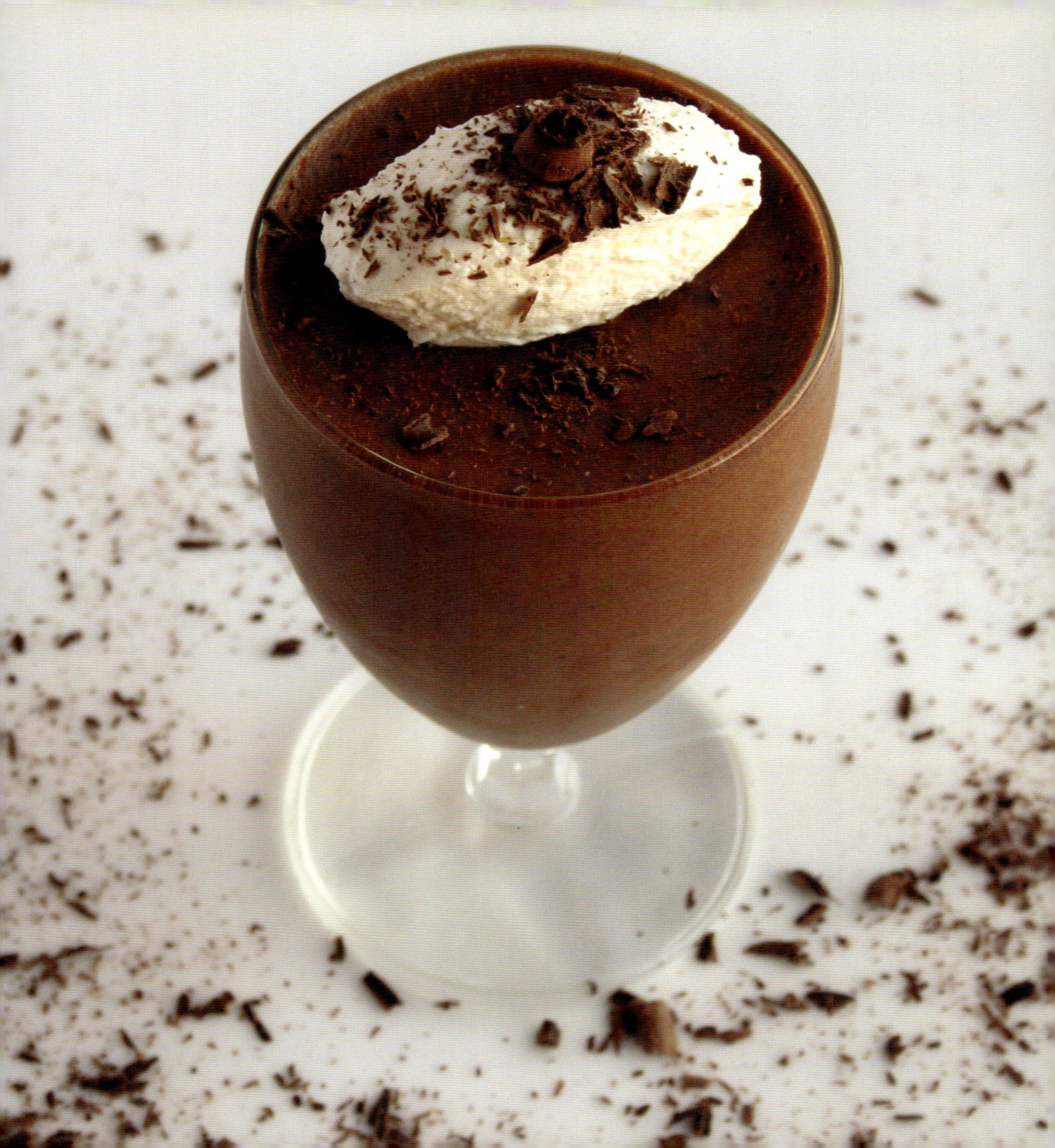

Triple Choc Brownies

Makes:	1 dozen brownies
Preparation:	30-35 mins
Cooking:	25-30 mins

300ml beer (dark) – chef's tip: Black Mac
1 cup all-purpose flour
¾ cup unsweetened cocoa powder
¼ teaspoon salt
85gm unsalted butter cut into small cubes
225gm dark chocolate chopped
135gm white chocolate chips
4 large eggs at room temperature
1 cup caster sugar
180gm semi-sweet chocolate chips
¼ cup icing sugar for dusting

Oven: preheat to 190°C.

Bowl 1: sift the flour, cocoa powder and salt into the bowl and mix well. Set aside.

Double boiler: using a double boiler, or a small pot with 3cm of water, bring to the boil and immediately reduce heat so the water simmers. Place a metal or glass bowl over the pot, making sure it does not touch the water. Combine the butter, dark chocolate and white chocolate chips in the bowl. Use the indirect heat to melt the chocolate, using a high-heat spatula to work the mixture until it is smooth. Remove from the heat.

Bowl 2 (large): beat the eggs and sugar until light and fluffy. Add the melted chocolate mix and stir until combined. Beat the flour mixture into the chocolate mixture and gradually add the beer (at room temperature), whisking all the time. Though the mixture may seem a bit thin, sprinkle the semi-sweet chocolate chips evenly across the surface. Some will sink but that's part of the plan.

Baking pan: pour the brownie mix into a pan lined with non-stick paper. Bake for 25-30 minutes or until an inserted skewer comes out almost clean. Remove, turn out on to a rack and allow to cool. Cut to size. Dust with icing sugar.

Brown Sugar Cookies

Makes:	40 cookies
Preparation:	10-15 mins
Cooking:	20 mins

150ml beer (dark) – chef's tip: Black Mac
½ cup brown sugar firmly packed
½ cup unsalted butter
2 cups all-purpose flour
½ teaspoon baking soda
1½ teaspoons ground cinnamon
½ cup walnuts halved

Oven: preheat to 175°C.

Bowl: cream the brown sugar and butter. Cut in the flour, baking soda and cinnamon. Gradually pour in the beer at room temperature to slowly form a soft dough.

Baking tray: create cookies by dropping dough in teaspoon-sized portions onto a greased baking tray and topping with a small amount of walnut.

Bake for about 20 minutes until lightly brown. Remove and cool on a rack.

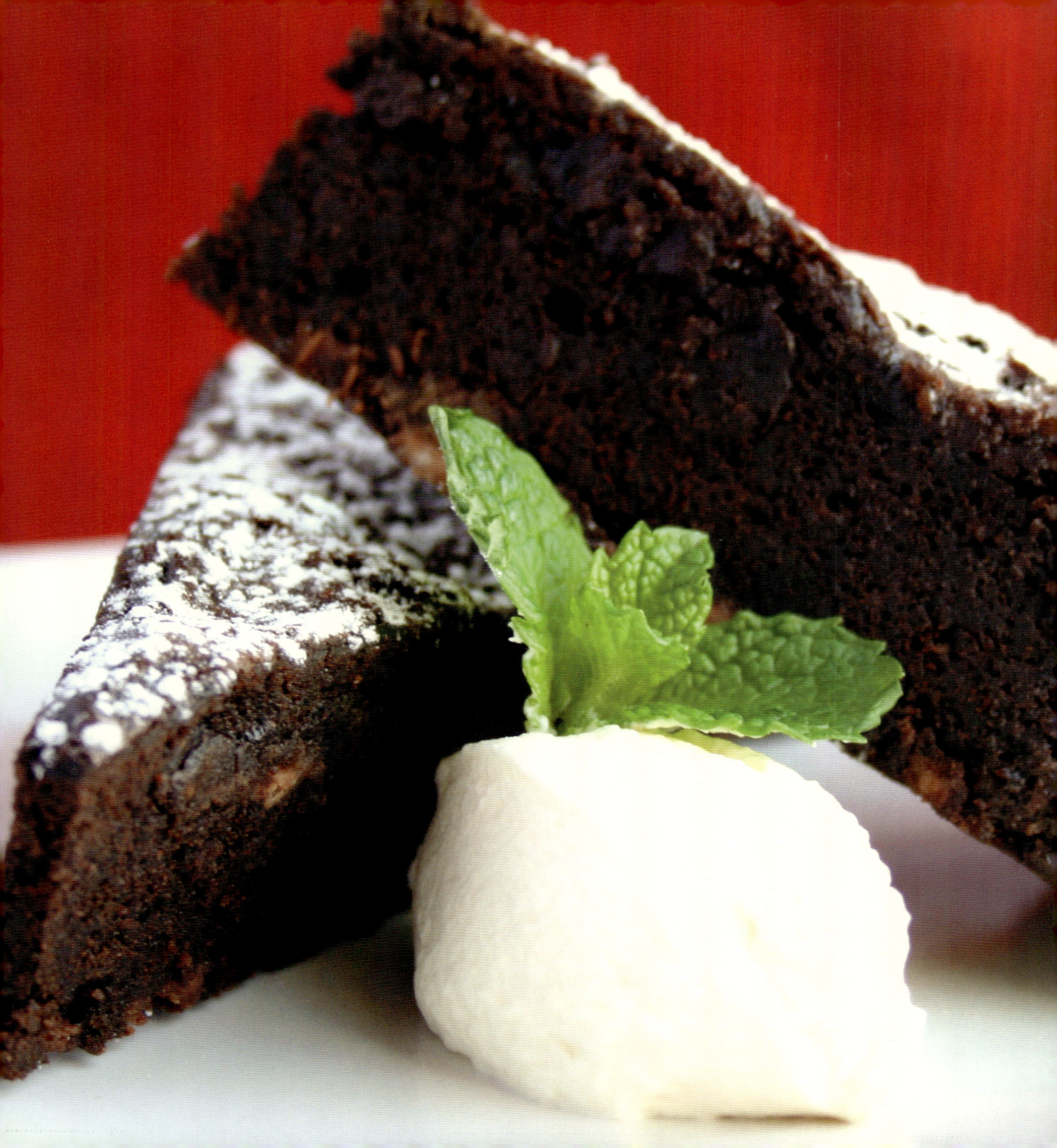

Chocolate Cheesecake

Serves:	12 portions
Preparation:	35-40 mins
Refrigeration:	overnight
Cooking:	1½-1¾ hours

180ml beer (dark) – chef's tip: Black Mac
1 cup plain biscuits crushed
2 tablespoons caster sugar
1 teaspoon unsweetened cocoa powder
55gm unsalted butter melted
675gm cream cheese softened
1 cup white sugar
3 eggs
225gm bitter-sweet chocolate chips
2 tablespoons cream
1 cup sour cream
Pinch of salt
2 teaspoons vanilla extract

Garnish

Grated chocolate

Oven: preheat to 180°C.

Springform pan (round, 22cm): grease the pan with butter. Wrap the outside of the pan with 3 or 4 layers of aluminium foil, ensuring that water can not get into the pan from outside.

Bowl 1 (small): mix the crushed biscuits, 2 tablespoons of sugar, cocoa and then add the butter. When the mixture is moist, press it into the bottom of the pan and firmly pack it down.

Bowl 2 (large): beat the cream cheese either manually or with an electric mixer until it is smooth. Gradually add the 1 cup of sugar and then one egg at a time, beating continuously to keep smooth.

Bowl 3 (microwave-safe): combine the chocolate chips and cream. Warm in the microwave until the chocolate is melted, ensuring it is not over-cooked.

Stir the chocolate into the large bowl (with the cream cheese mix). Add the sour cream, beer, salt and vanilla. Beat until smooth.

Pour this mixture over the crust in the base of the springform pan.

Baking dish (large, ovenproof): sit the springform pan inside this larger dish. Half fill the larger dish with boiling water to create a water bath. Place in the middle of your oven.

Oven: bake the cheesecake for 45 minutes. Turn off the oven and leave to rest in the oven, with its door slightly open, for 1 hour more. Remove from the oven and use a knife to loosen the edge of the cheesecake from the springform pan.

Refrigerate overnight to chill and set the cheesecake.

Serving up

Sprinkle grated chocolate across the top of the cheesecake.

Chocolate Waffles

Makes:	about 5
Preparation:	10-15 mins
Cooking:	3-5 mins each

60ml beer (dark) – chef's tip: Speight's Old Dark
1½ cups self-raising flour
2 tablespoons cocoa
3 tablespoons caster sugar
½ teaspoon salt
2 medium eggs separated
1¼ cups cream
1½ tablespoons unsalted butter melted
30gm white chocolate chips

Bowl 1: sift the flour, cocoa, sugar and salt into the bowl. Mix well.

Bowl 2: beat the egg yolks. Add the cream and mix. Combine this mixture with the dry ingredients in Bowl 1. Stir in the melted butter. Add the beer, mixing well.

Bowl 3: beat the egg whites with an electric mixer until stiff and fold them into the batter. Fold in the white chocolate chips.

Waffle iron: cook the waffles for 3-5 minutes in your waffle iron, until they are to your liking.

Serving up

Serve with ice cream.

Banana Waffles

Makes:	about 10
Preparation:	10-15 mins
Cooking:	3-5 mins each

125ml beer (lager) – chef's tip: Export Gold
2¼ cups all-purpose flour
2½ teaspoons baking powder
¼ teaspoon salt
4 tablespoons caster sugar
½ teaspoon ground nutmeg
3 medium eggs separated
1 cup milk
125gm unsalted butter melted
2 bananas thinly sliced

Bowl 1 (large): sift in the flour, baking powder, salt, sugar and ground nutmeg. Mix well.

Bowl 2: beat the egg yolks. Add the milk and mix. Combine this mixture with the dry ingredients in Bowl 1. Stir in the melted butter. Add the beer, mixing well.

Bowl 3: beat the egg whites with an electric mixer until stiff and fold them into the batter. Fold in the banana slices.

Waffle iron: cook the waffles for 3-5 minutes in your waffle iron, until they are to your liking.

Serving up

Serve with bacon and pancake syrup (see recipe on page 139).

Afghan Biscuits with Beer Icing

Makes:	14 biscuits
Preparation:	10-15 mins
Cooking:	15-20 mins

200gm unsalted butter (room temperature)
½ cup caster sugar
3 tablespoons cocoa powder
1¼ cups all-purpose flour
1¼ cups cornflakes
14 walnut halves

Icing

80ml beer (dark) – chef's tip: Black Mac
120gm butter
3½ cups icing sugar
5½ tablespoons cocoa powder

Oven: preheat to 180°C.

Bowl: to make the biscuits, cream the 200gm of butter and caster sugar until light and fluffy. Sift in the 3 tablespoons of cocoa and the flour. Fold in the cornflakes, mixing well.

Use tablespoons of the mix to form biscuit shapes, pressing the mixture together. Lay out your biscuits on a greased baking tray and bake for about 15 minutes or until the biscuits are set.

Bowl: to make the icing, cream the 120gm of butter with half of the icing sugar. Add the 5½ tablespoons of cocoa and some of the beer. Beat until smooth and alternatively add portions of the icing sugar and beer. Keep beating until you have a fluffy mixture of icing consistency.

Spread over the cooled baked biscuits and top with a walnut half.

Jaffa Cake

Serves:	4
Preparation:	15-20 mins
Cooking:	35-40 mins

150ml beer (dark) – chef's tip: Speight's Old Dark
225gm unsalted butter softened
225gm brown sugar firmly packed
4 eggs
275gm self-raising flour
1 teaspoon baking powder
1 pinch salt
2 tablespoons cocoa powder
Juice and zest of 1 orange
2 drops orange essence
110gm butter softened
225gm icing sugar

Oven: preheat to 185°C.

Bowl 1: cream the 225gm of butter and sugar until light and fluffy. Add the eggs one at a time, mixing well after each egg. Sift in the flour, baking powder, salt and cocoa. Add half the zest from the orange and the orange essence and beat the mixture well. Gradually fold in the beer, mixing well but without over-beating.

Cake tins: pour the mixture into two greased cake tins and smooth down. Bake for 35-40 minutes or until the cakes are springy to touch. Remove and cool on a rack.

Bowl 2: to make the icing, cream the 110gm of butter and icing sugar in a bowl. Blend in the remaining orange zest and sufficient juice to make an icing that is smooth and consistent.

When cool, ice the tops of each cake and place on top of each other to form one cake.

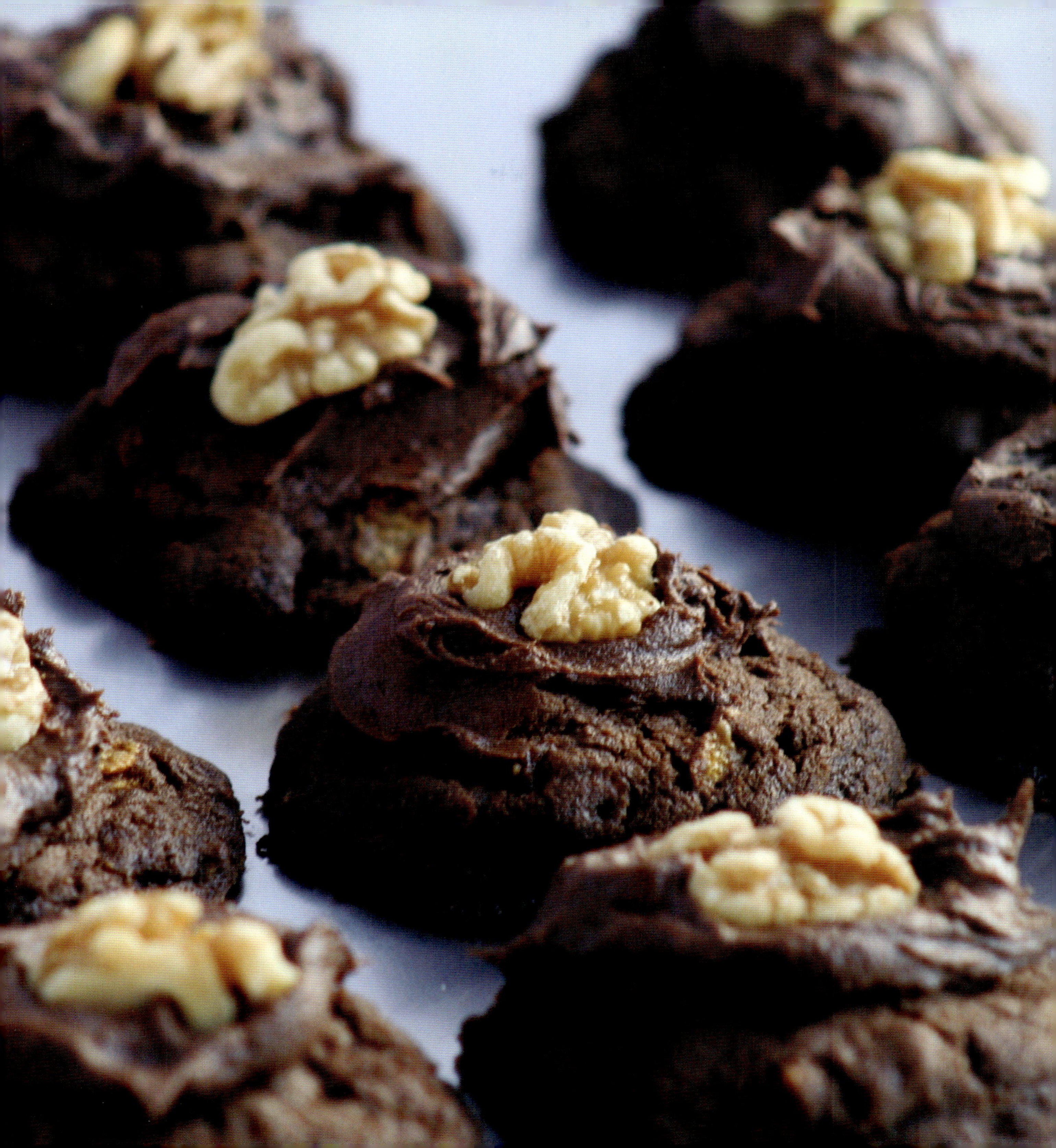

Chocolate Malt Ice Cream

Makes:	about 1 litre
Preparation:	5-10 mins
Cooking:	25-30 mins

330ml beer (malt) – chef's tip: Speight's Old Dark
1 tablespoon unsweetened cocoa powder
½ vanilla bean
5 egg yolks
2 cups cream
2 cups milk
¾ cup sugar

Saucepan 1: boil the beer in a saucepan over medium-high heat. Maintain the heat while it reduces to about half its original volume. If it froths, take off the heat for a few seconds before returning it to the heat.

Allow the beer to cool for 3-5 minutes. Whisk in the cocoa powder. Split the vanilla bean and scrape the seeds into the mix, adding the empty pod. Set aside.

Bowl 1 (large, metal): make an ice bath by half-filling a large steel bowl with water and ice. Set aside.

Bowl 2 (medium): make creme anglais by whisking the egg yolks.

Saucepan 2: combine the cream, milk and sugar and slowly bring to the boil over a medium heat. As soon as boiling point is reached, gradually pour this mix into the bowl of yolks, whisking all the time. When combined, return this mix to the saucepan and heat over low-medium heat. Stir constantly until the mixture thickens and forms a coat on the back of a wooden spoon.

Bowl 3 (medium, metal): strain the creme anglais through a fine strainer into a metal bowl.

Strain the beer mixture into the same bowl, removing the vanilla pod.

Whisk the beer and cream mixtures together. Place the metal bowl in the ice bath, allowing it to cool the mixture while you continue to stir for 5-7 more minutes.

If you have an ice cream maker, follow the manufacturer's instructions. If not, you can make the ice cream by using the following method.

Transfer the bowl to a freezer for 20 minutes. Remove and stir. Freeze for 20 more minutes and stir again. Freeze for a third period of 20 minutes and stir once more. Freeze until set.

Pikelets

Makes:	16
Preparation:	10-15 mins
Cooking:	20-25 mins

370ml beer (lager) – chef's tip: Steinlager Pure
2 cups all-purpose flour
½ cup white sugar
1½ teaspoons baking powder
½ teaspoon salt
2 eggs beaten
4 tablespoons unsalted butter melted

Bowl: sift the flour, sugar, baking powder and salt into the bowl and mix well. Pour in the beaten eggs, melted butter and beer. Whisk together until blended.

Fry pan: heat a non-stick fry pan over medium heat and coat with vegetable oil spray.

Spoon about ¼ cup of batter onto the hot surface to make each pancake.

When bubbles appear on the top of the pancakes, flip. Cook until browned on both sides.

Serving up

Serve with pancake syrup – see below.

Pancake Syrup

Makes:	1 cup
Preparation:	5 mins
Cooking:	5-10 mins

125ml beer (lager) – chef's tip: Export Gold
1½ cups brown sugar firmly packed
½ teaspoon ground cinnamon
45gm unsalted butter

Saucepan: combine all the ingredients in a saucepan and heat over medium heat. Gradually bring to a boil and remove from heat.

Serving up

Serve slightly warm or at room temperature. Try over vanilla ice cream, with waffles or pancakes.

Chocolate-dipped Strawberries

Makes:	1-1½ punnets
Preparation:	5 mins
Refrigeration:	1 hour minimum
Cooking:	5-10 mins

30ml beer (dark) – chef's tip: Black Mac
100gm chocolate
1-1½ punnets strawberries
Shredded coconut (optional)
Toasted almonds chopped (optional)

Double boiler: using a double boiler, or a small pot with 3cm of water, bring to the boil and immediately reduce heat so the water simmers. Place a metal or glass bowl over the pot, making sure it does not touch the water.

Break the chocolate into pieces and combine with the beer in the bowl. Use the indirect heat to melt the chocolate with the beer, using a high-heat spatula to work the mixture until it is smooth.

Remove from the heat and dip your strawberries in as deep as you like. Place them on baking paper and if you wish, sprinkle some or all with shredded coconut or chopped toasted almonds.

Refrigerate for at least 1 hour to make sure they are set, then serve.

Spice Cake

Serves:	6-8
Preparation:	30-40 mins
Cooking:	1-1¼ hours

330ml beer (lager) – chef's tip: Moneith's Golden
1½ cups brown sugar firmly packed
150gm soft unsalted butter
2 eggs
2½ cups all-purpose flour
1½ teaspoons baking powder
½ teaspoon baking soda
¼ teaspoon salt
1 teaspoon ground cinnamon
1 teaspoon ground allspice
1 teaspoon ground cloves
½ cup raisins
½ cup walnuts chopped

Oven: preheat your oven to 175°C.

Bowl 1: combine the sugar and soft butter in a bowl, creaming well until light and fluffy. Beat in the eggs, one at a time. Blend well.

Bowl 2: sift the flour, baking powder, baking soda, salt, cinnamon, allspice and cloves, mixing well. Add this mixture to the egg mixture. Gradually add the beer, mixing well. Stir in the raisins and walnuts. Mix well.

Ring tin: pour the cake mix into a greased ring tin.

Oven: bake for 1 hour or until a skewer inserted into the cake emerges clean. Remove the ring tin and allow to cool for about 10 minutes. Remove the cake from the tin and leave to cool on a rack.

Top with your favourite icing or enjoy it plain.

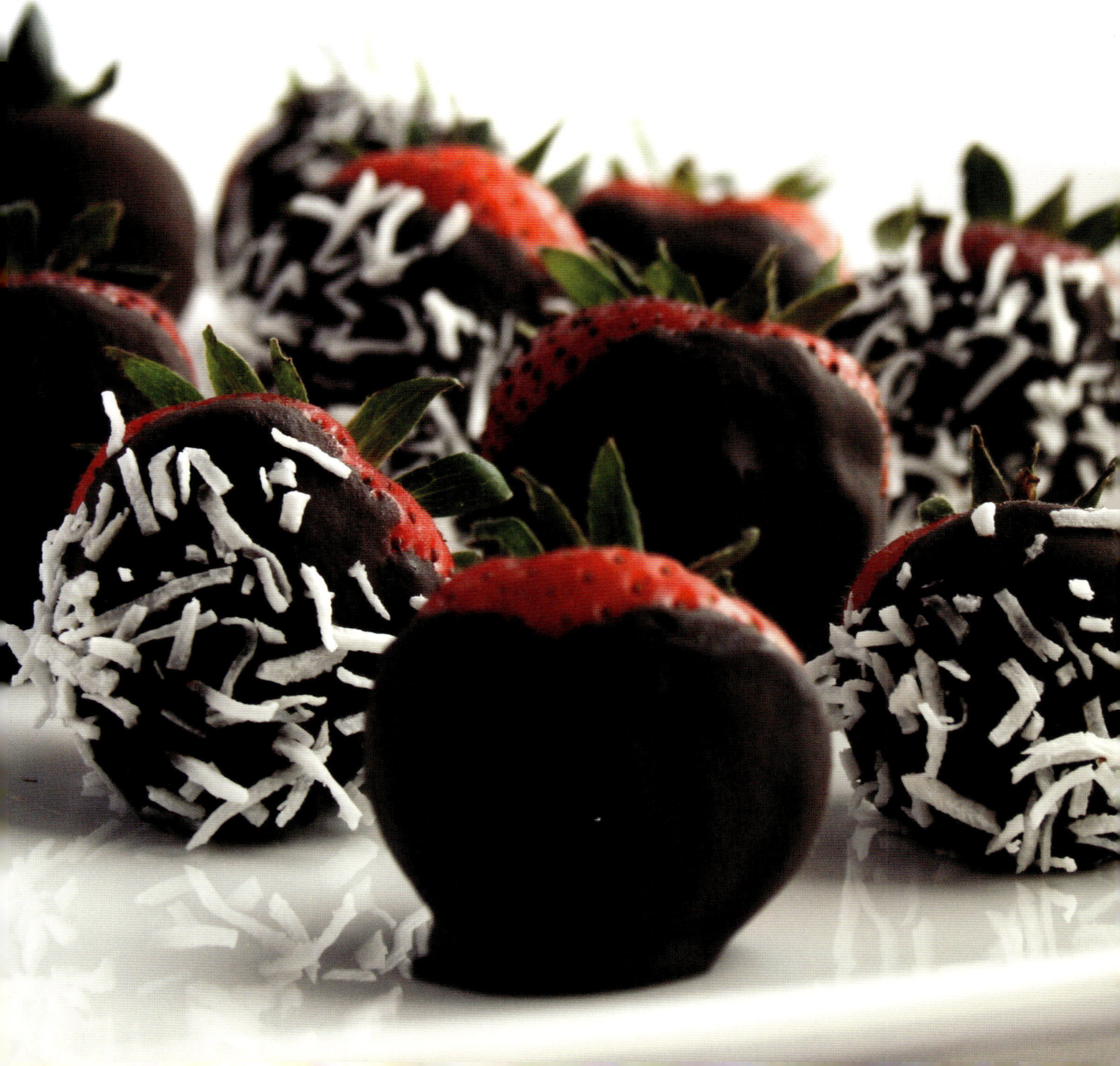

Index of contents

A
Afghan Biscuits with Beer Icing, 136
Aioli, 64
Almond-crusted Trout Fillets, 84
Apple Crumble, 129
Asian-style Salmon, 88
Asparagus Risotto, 55
Avocado Wedges, 18

B
Bacon Hock & Vegetable Soup, 43
Banana Waffles, 135
Banana, Date & Walnut Bread, 38
Basil Bread, 24
Batter
   Avocado Wedges, 18
   Fish, 85
   Fish in Beer & Vodka Batter, 86
   Onion Rings, 58
   Oysters, 80
   Sesame Green Beans, 52
   Vegetables, 58
Bean Dip, 10
Bearnaise Sauce, 68
Beef
   Beef & Kumara Casserole, 104
   Beef & Vegetable Stew, 105
   Beef, Mushroom & Bacon Pie, 118
   Beef Stir-fry, 123
   Beef Stroganoff, 100
   Burger & Onions, 122
   Corned Silverside, 112
   Dry Beef Curry, 119
   Garlic Roast Beef, 126
   Herb Steak Marinade, 73
   Lime Steak Marinade, 72
   Shepherd's Pie, 116
   Soy & Ginger Steak Marinade, 72
   Spag Bol, 125
   Steak Pie, 111
Beef & Kumara Casserole, 104
Beef & Vegetable Stew, 105
Beef, Mushroom & Bacon Pie, 118
Beef Stir-fry, 123
Beef Stroganoff, 100
Beer Batter Fish, 85
Beer Batter Onion Rings, 58
Beer Batter Vegetables, 58
Beer Can Chicken, 120
Black Bean & Chorizo Soup, 50
Blue Cheese Dip, 8
Blue Cheese Sauce, 68
Braised Cabbage, 54
Bran Muffins, 35
Breads
   Banana, Date & Walnut, 38
   Basil, 24
   Cheese & Onion, 24
   Fruit & Raisin, 36
   Herb, 26
   Pepperoni, 32
   Rye, 25
   Savoury Swirl, 26
   Sourdough, 28-29
   Sun-dried Tomato, 25
   Whole Wheat, 22
   World's Easiest Bread, 22
Broccoli & Blue Cheese Soup, 47
Brown Sugar Cookies, 132
Brussels Sprouts, 60
Burger & Onions, 122

C
Cakes
   Chocolate Cheesecake, 134
   Chocolate Chip & Walnut, 129
   Cocoa, 128
   Jaffa, 136
   Spice, 140
   Tipsy Fruitcake, 128
Carrots, 54
Casseroles
   Beef & Kumara, 104
   Kiwi, 101
   Sausage, 96
Cheese
   Blue Cheese Dip, 8
   Blue Cheese Sauce, 68
   Broccoli & Blue Cheese Soup, 47
   Cheese & Onion Bread, 24
   Cheese & Onion Dip, 12
   Cheese & Spinach Dip, 9
   Classic Cheese on Toast, 13
   Fondue, 12
   Macaroni with Bacon, 125
   Muffins, 34
Cheese & Onion Bread, 24
Cheese & Onion Dip, 12
Cheese & Spinach Dip, 9
Cheese Fondue, 12
Cheese Muffins, 34
Chicken
   Beer Can Chicken, 120
   Chilli Stew, 106
   Curried Tomato Chicken, 112
   Grilled Chicken Satay, 17
   Jambalaya, 115
   Kiwi Casserole, 101
   Paella, 110
   Roast Herb Chicken, 114
   Wings with Salsa, 16
Chicken Chilli Stew, 106
Chicken Paella, 110
Chicken Wings with Salsa, 16
Chilli
   Chicken Chilli Stew, 106
   Pumpkin, Pear & Chilli Soup, 40
   Venison Chilli, 98
Chocolate
   Afghan Biscuits, 136
   Cheesecake, 134
   Chocolate Chip & Walnut Cake, 129
   Cocoa Cake, 128
   Dipped strawberries, 140
   Jaffa Cake, 136
   Malt Ice Cream, 138
   Mousse, 130
   Triple Choc Brownies, 132
   Truffles, 130
   Waffles, 135
Chocolate Cheesecake, 134
Chocolate Chip & Walnut Cake, 129
Chocolate Malt Ice Cream, 138
Chocolate Mousse, 130
Chocolate Truffles, 130
Chocolate Waffles, 135
Chocolate-dipped Strawberries, 140
Classic Cheese on Toast, 13
Cocktail Sauce, 66
Cocoa Cake, 128
Coleslaw, 62
Corn Fritters, 20
Corned Silverside, 112
Crab Dip, 8
Cream of Mushroom Soup, 40
Crumbed Venison Steaks, 114
Curried Tomato Chicken, 112
Curry
   Dry Beef, 119
   Kumara & Curried Apple Soup, 42
   Lamb Rogan Josh, 119
   Tomato Chicken, 112

D
Deviled Eggs, 18
Dips
   Aioli, 64
   Bean, 10
   Blue Cheese, 8
   Cheese & Onion, 12
   Cheese & Spinach, 9
   Crab, 8
   Kumara & Coriander, 9
   Prawns with Yoghurt Dip, 82
Dry Beef Curry, 119
Duck Stew, 97

E
Eggs
   Deviled Eggs, 18
   Smoked Salmon with Scrambled Eggs, 92

F
Fish
   Almond-crusted Trout, 84
   Asian-style Salmon, 88
   Beer Batter Fish, 85
   Boil Up, 90
   - in Beer & Vodka Batter, 86
   Poached Salmon, 81
   Saffron Fish Stew, 89
   Seafood Gumbo, 46
   Teriyaki, 88
Fish Boil Up, 90

Fish in Beer & Vodka Batter, 86
Fruit & Raisin Bread, 36

G
Garlic & Herb Butter, 69
Garlic Prawns, 82
Garlic Roast Beef, 126
Grilled Chicken Satay, 17

H
Herb Bread, 26
Herb Steak Marinade, 73

J
Jaffa Cake, 136
Jambalaya, 115

K
Kiwi Casserole, 101
Kumara & Coriander Dip, 9
Kumara & Curried Apple Soup, 42
Kumara & Pineapple Salad, 59

L
Lamb Marinade, 74
Lamb Rogan Josh, 119
Lamb Shanks, 108
Leek & Potato Soup, 47
Lime Steak Marinade, 72

M
Macaroni Cheese with Bacon, 125
Marinades
    Herb Steak, 73
    Lamb, 74
    Lime Steak, 72
    Salmon, 73
    Soy & Ginger Steak, 72
    Venison, 74
Muffins
    Bran, 35
    Cheese, 34
    Oatmeal, 34
    Savoury, 35
Mushroom & Barley, 55
Mushroom Platter, 14
Mussels with Salsa, 78

O
Oatmeal Muffins, 34
Onion Gravy, 70
Onion Soup, 44
Oxtail Stew, 94
Oyster & Watercress Risotto, 80
Oysters, 80

P
Pancake Syrup, 139
Pasta
    Macaroni Cheese with Bacon, 125
    Pizza & Pasta Sauce, 76
    Spag Bol, 125
Pepperoni Bread, 32
Pies
    Beef, Mushroom & Bacon, 118
    Shepherd's, 116
    Steak, 111
Pikelets, 139
Pizza & Pasta Sauce, 76
Pizza Crust, 30
Poached Salmon, 81
Pork Basting Sauce, 70
Pork Boil Up, 105
Pork Stew, 106
Potato Layer Cake, 62
Potato Salad, 59
Prawn Fritters, 20
Prawns with Yoghurt Dip, 82
Pumpkin, Pear & Chilli Soup, 40

R
Ratatouille, 56
Roast Herb Chicken, 114
Roast Tomato & Garlic Soup, 48
Roasted Asparagus with Hollandaise Sauce, 60
Rye Bread, 25

S
Saffron Fish Stew, 89
Salads
    Coleslaw, 62
    Kumara & Pineapple, 59
    Potato, 59
Salmon Marinade, 73
Salsa, 14
Satay Sauce, 65
Sauces
    Aioli, 64
    Bearnaise, 68
    Blue Cheese, 68
    Cocktail, 66
    Garlic & Herb Butter, 69
    Hollandaise, 60
    Onion Gravy, 70
    Pancake Syrup, 139
    Pizza & Pasta, 76
    Pork Basting, 70
    Salsa, 14
    Satay, 65
    Sweet Bacon, 69
    Sweet Mustard, 64
    Tangy Tomato, 65
    Tartare, 66
Sausage Casserole, 96
Sausages & Capsicum Stew, 102
Sausages & Garlic Mash, 124
Savoury Muffins, 35
Savoury Swirl Bread, 26
Seafood Gumbo, 46
Sesame Green Beans, 52
Shellfish
    Chorizo Mussels, 78
    Fish Boil Up, 90
    Garlic Prawns, 82
    Jambalaya, 115
    Mussels with Salsa, 78
    Oysters, 80
    Prawn Fritters, 20
    Prawns with Yoghurt Dip, 82
    Saffron Fish Stew, 89
    Seafood Gumbo, 46
    Steamed Crayfish, 81
    Steamed Pipis or Cockles with Bacon, 85
Shepherd's Pie, 116
Smoked Salmon with Scrambled Eggs, 92
Sourdough Bread, 28-29
Soups
    Bacon Hock & Vegetable, 43
    Black Bean & Chorizo, 50
    Broccoli & Blue Cheese, 47
    Cream of Mushroom, 40
    Kumara & Curried Apple, 42
    Leek & Potato, 47
    Onion, 44
    Pumpkin, Pear & Chilli, 40
    Roast Tomato & Garlic, 48
    Seafood Gumbo, 46
Soy & Ginger Steak Marinade, 72
Spag Bol, 125
Spice Cake, 140
Steak Pie, 111
Steamed Crayfish, 81
Steamed Pipis or Cockles with Bacon, 85
Stews
    Beef & Vegetable, 105
    Beef Stroganoff, 100
    Chicken Chilli, 106
    Duck, 97
    Fish Boil Up, 90
    Oxtail, 94
    Pork, 106
    Pork Boil Up, 105
    Saffron Fish Stew, 89
    Sausages & Capsicum, 102
Stuffed Tomatoes, 13
Sun-dried Tomato Bread, 25
Sweet Bacon Sauce, 69
Sweet Mustard Sauce, 64

T
Tangy Tomato Sauce, 65
Tartare Sauce, 66
Teriyaki Fish, 88
Tipsy Fruitcake, 128
Triple Choc Brownies, 132

V
Vegetable Stir-fry, 52
Vegetables
    Asparagus Risotto, 55
    Bacon Hock & Vegetable Stew, 43
    Beer Batter Vegetables, 58
    Braised Cabbage, 54
    Brussels Sprouts, 60
    Carrots, 54
    Coleslaw, 62
    Ratatouille, 56
    Sesame Green Beans, 52
    Stir-fry, 52
Venison Chilli, 98
Venison Marinade, 74

W
Whole Wheat Bread, 22
World's Easiest Bread, 22

About the chef

Sam Cook is the pen name for an experienced Kiwi chef who has plied his trade at restaurants in New Zealand, Australia and the United Kingdom. He shuns celebrity chef status, believing the focus should be on the food and not the chef. He also likes a beer.